Lexical Innovation in World Englishes

Lexical Innovation in World Englishes contributes to the investigation of World Englishes by offering insights into the lexical developments of selected English varieties and their cross-fertilization potential. Taking a theoretical and empirical approach and focusing on neological formations, this book:

- discusses and problematizes different categorizations of English varieties and processes of word formation, considering the expansion of English across the world;
- draws on authentic examples taken from language corpora to gain a finer understanding of the varieties' transformations and of their reciprocal influences from a lexical perspective;
- aims to validate general considerations on the lexical features of these varieties of English and test them using corpora.

Including eight empirical case studies, this innovative text shows the importance of investigating lexical developments to observe the evolution of a variety while arguing for the need to go beyond a purely structuralist approach and to include a broader discursive and sociological perspective. *Lexical Innovation in World Englishes* is key reading for postgraduate students and researchers in the fields of World Englishes and language varieties.

Patrizia Anesa is a lecturer at the University of Bergamo, Italy.

Lexical Innovation in World Englishes
Cross-fertilization and Evolving Paradigms

Patrizia Anesa

LONDON AND NEW YORK

First published 2019 by Routledge

2 Park Square, Milton Park, Abingdon, Oxon OX14 4RN
605 Third Avenue, New York, NY 10017

Routledge is an imprint of the Taylor & Francis Group, an informa business

First issued in paperback 2022

Copyright © 2019 Patrizia Anesa

The right of Patrizia Anesa to be identified as author of this work has been asserted by her in accordance with sections 77 and 78 of the Copyright, Designs and Patents Act 1988.

All rights reserved. No part of this book may be reprinted or reproduced or utilised in any form or by any electronic, mechanical, or other means, now known or hereafter invented, including photocopying and recording, or in any information storage or retrieval system, without permission in writing from the publishers.

Notice:
Product or corporate names may be trademarks or registered trademarks, and are used only for identification and explanation without intent to infringe.

Publisher's Note

The publisher has gone to great lengths to ensure the quality of this reprint but points out that some imperfections in the original copies may be apparent.

British Library Cataloguing-in-Publication Data
A catalogue record for this book is available from the British Library

Library of Congress Cataloging-in-Publication Data
Names: Anesa, Patrizia, 1982- author.
Title: Lexical innovation in world Englishes : cross-fertilization and evolving paradigms / Patrizia Anesa.
Description: London ; New York, NY : Routledge, 2018. | Series: Routledge focus on linguistics | Includes bibliographical references and index.
Identifiers: LCCN 2018019718| ISBN 9780815363453 (hardback) | ISBN 9781351109352 (e-book)
Subjects: LCSH: English language—New words. | English language—Word formation. | English language—Foreign countries.
Classification: LCC PE1583 .A525 2018 | DDC 422—dc23
LC record available at https://lccn.loc.gov/2018019718

ISBN: 978-0-815-36345-3 (hbk)
ISBN: 978-1-03-233900-9 (pbk)
DOI: 10.4324/9781351109352

Typeset in Times New Roman
by Swales & Willis Ltd, Exeter, Devon, UK

To Francesco

Contents

Acknowledgments x
List of figures xi
List of tables xii
List of abbreviations xiii

PART 1 1

1 Introduction 3

1.1 Scope and aims 3
1.2 Focus 5
1.3 Structure of the book 7

2 Investigating English and Englishes 10

2.1 Definitional issues 11
2.2 Categorizations and their limitations 14
2.3 Nativeness 23
2.4 Standard(s) in language 25
    2.4.1 English standards 26
    2.4.2 Defining standard varieties 27
    2.4.3 Pidgins and creoles 28
2.5 The World Englishes ethos 30

PART 2 33

3 Lexical developments 35

3.1 Productivity and creativity 36
3.2 Investigating neologisms 38
3.3 From nonce-formations to neologisms 40

4 Word-formation processes 45

4.1 Composites 47
   4.1.1 Affixation 47
   4.1.2 Compounding 48
4.2 Abbreviations 48
   4.2.1 Acronyms and initialisms 49
   4.2.2 Clipping 49
4.3 Blends 49
4.4 Borrowing 50
4.5 Conversion 51
4.6 Semantic drift 51
4.7 Eponyms 52

5 Methodological approach 53

5.1 Approaches to the study of neologisms 53
5.2 Corpora 54
5.3 Lexicographic resources 60
5.4 Research approach 62

PART 3 67

6 Case studies 69

6.1 English in Africa 69
   6.1.1 Nigerian English 70
   6.1.2 East Africa 80
   6.1.3 South Africa 84
6.2 Varieties in Asia 88
   6.2.1 Singapore 90
   6.2.2 Hong Kong 100
   6.2.3 The Philippines 103
   6.2.4 India 109
6.3 Caribbean English 115
   6.3.1 Contact languages and beyond 115
   6.3.2 Jamaican English 116
6.4 Towards a macrovarietal approach? 120
6.5 WE lexicographic labels 122

7 Conclusions 127

7.1 Evolving paradigms 128
7.2 Creativity and innovation 129
7.3 Final implications 131

Appendix 1	134
Appendix 2	136
References	139
Index	153

Acknowledgments

I am indebted to many people who have directly, or indirectly, contributed to the creation of this book, whether through their comments and their suggestions, or by the incredible amount of time they decided to share with me in order to discuss the contents of this work. Any errors or omissions remain, obviously, solely my responsibility.

I am particularly grateful to my colleagues and students at the University of Bergamo, for their precious help, for being so inspiring, and because the intellectually enriching exchanges that we had substantially contributed to this work. My thanks also go to the editorial staff at Routledge for their enthusiasm, patience, and the scrupulous attention they have devoted to this project throughout its different phases.

This acknowledgement would be incomplete if I failed to thank my family and friends for their constant and immeasurable support. Francesco, Fernanda, and Lorenzo are in this book more than they know, as nothing I have done would have been the same without them.

Finally, dear Francesco, thank you for teaching me that the best things in life are not things. I know you are probably smiling somewhere, thinking I have produced another incomprehensible piece of writing.

Figures

2.1	Levels of English in the world	19
2.2	Englishes and their permeability	20
2.3	English transnational polycentrism	21
2.4	Traditional life cycle of a creole	29
3.1	Potential stages of the life cycle of a word	41
5.1	Varieties analyzed	62
5.2	Methodological quadrangulation	65

Tables

2.1	World System of Standard and Non-standard Englishes	15
5.1	ICE corpus design	56
5.2	GloWbE outline	57
5.3	Raw frequencies of lexical items and log-likelihood value (INE)	59
5.4	Raw frequencies of lexical items and log-likelihood value (SGE)	59
5.5	Raw frequencies of lexical items and log-likelihood value (HKE)	60
6.1	Frequency of *bwana* in GloWbE	81
6.2	Frequency of *uhuru* in GloWbE	82
6.3	Neologisms in SAE	86
6.4	Frequency of *braai* in GloWbE	88
6.5	Word-formation processes in PHE and SGE	89
6.6	Usages of *makan* in CSGE	94
6.7	Frequency of *-cum-* constructions in GloWbE	97
6.8	Examples of Chinese borrowings	101
6.9	Frequency of *guanxi* in GloWbE	102
6.10	Frequency of *wet market* in GloWbE	103
6.11	Frequency of *kuya* in GloWbE	105
6.12	Frequency of *comfort room* in GloWbE	107
6.13	Frequency of *jeepney* in GloWbE	108
6.14	Frequency of *brinjal* in GloWbE	110
6.15	Lexical items in PHE, SGE, and MYE	122
6.16	Dictionary 'labels' for WE lexical items	123

Abbreviations

AmE	American English
ASEAN	Association of Southeast Asian Nations
AU	Australia
AUE	Australian English
BD	Bangladesh
BDE	Bangladesh English
BrE	British English
BSAE	Black South African English
CA	Canada
CCJ	Corpus of Cyber-Jamaican
CD	Collins English Dictionary (online)
CEDO	Cambridge English Dictionary Online
CSGE	Colloquial Singapore English
EA	East Africa
EAE	East African English
EFL	English as a Foreign Language
EIF	Extra- and Intra-territorial Forces
ELF	English as a Lingua Franca
ENL	English as a Native Language
ESL	English as a Second Language
GB	Great Britain
GH	Ghana
GHE	Ghanian English
GloWbE	Corpus of Global Web-based English
HK	Hong Kong
HKE	Hong Kong English
ICE	International Corpus of English
IE	Ireland
IN	India
INE	Indian English

JC	Jamaican Creole
JE	Jamaican English
JM	Jamaica
KE	Kenya
KEE	Kenyan English
LK	Sri Lanka
MD	Macquarie Dictionary Online
MMD	Macmillan Dictionary (online)
MW	Merriam-Webster's Learner's Dictionary Online
MY	Malaysia
MYE	Malaysian English
NE	Nigerian English
NG	Nigeria
NPE	Nigerian Pidgin English
NZ	New Zealand
OALD	Oxford Advanced Learner's Dictionary Online
ODE	Oxforddictionaries.com
OED	*Oxford English Dictionary*
PCE	Postcolonial Englishes
PH	Philippines
PHE	Philippine English
PK	Pakistan
PKE	Pakistan English
SA	South Africa
SACOD	*South African Concise Oxford Dictionary*
SAE	South African English
SG	Singapore
SGE	Singapore English
SSGE	Standard Singapore English
TZ	Tanzania
TZE	Tanzanian English
WAVE	West African Vernacular English
WE	World Englishes
WIE	World International English
WSAE	White South African English
WSE	World Standard English
WW	WorldWeb Online Dictionary

Part 1

1 Introduction

1.1 Scope and aims

In recent decades, world varieties of English have received an ever-increasing level of scholarly attention. The body of research available on the topic is so extensive that any attempt at citing the relevant work is inevitably selective rather than representative. A wide range of approaches has been adopted, focusing, for example, on the historical developments of English varieties (Graddol/Leith/Swann 1996), their linguistic characteristics (Kortmann et al. 2004), or the social implications related to their use (Sharma 2011).

However, several works have often been guided by the desire to pinpoint the distinctive features of a variety by making use of methodologies which do not rest on any specific theory of language (Mahboob/Liang 2014). The very identification of English varieties is also frequently based on theoretical limitations, such as the coincidence of national borders with language boundaries. In this regard, Saraceni aptly notes that a crucial problematic aspect is the adoption of a perspective on language which stems from past nation-state ideologies, and which conceives "each language as a bounded system inextricably and primordially connected to a specific nation" (Saraceni 2014: 260). Although traditional varietal labels (such as Indian English or Nigerian English) will also be employed in this work for the sake of clarity, the main objective is to try to show the evolution of traditional varietal paradigms and to observe the phenomenon of cross-contamination.

This book focuses on lexical aspects of varieties of English with particular attention devoted to neological formations. Among the several approaches available when investigating the lexicon of a language, the emphasis on neologisms allows us to gain a more detailed understanding of lexical developments. It also enables us to discuss the level of productivity and creativity present in different varieties, as well as the reciprocal lexical influences which emerge.

4   *Introduction*

More specifically, this study contributes to the investigation of World Englishes (WE) by offering insights into the lexical aspects of selected varieties. The Englishes observed present a vast array of neologisms, which are revealing elements in linguistic analysis in that they manifestly represent the dynamic aspect of a language, and mirror social mutations (see Aitchison 2005; Crystal 2006; Labov 2006).

In this respect, it should be pointed out that Web 2.0 technologies have led to considerable changes in language usage in that, for example, new word formations may spread and reach a high level of frequency (thus being perceived as widely acceptable by a vast range of speakers) before they have been entered into a dictionary. Moreover, technological changes have also been credited in some cases as being sources of the democratization of language usage.

This work has both a theoretical and an empirical focus. Theoretically, it aims to discuss and problematize different categorizations of World English varieties and to present word-formation processes in light of the global expansion of English. Empirically, it aims to validate general considerations on the lexical features of selected varieties, testing them through the use of corpora and lexicographic resources. Although language corpora may be employed for the study of a wide range of features (e.g. linguistic, textual, and pragmatic), their usage is here restricted to the investigation of lexical aspects, the study of which has long benefited from such tools. Thus, this book aims to provide a concise and up-to-date investigation of the developments and advancements in morphological theory, as well as considerations regarding the societal implications embodied in word-formation processes across the varieties discussed. The analysis is based on lexical features which are distinctive of a particular variety of English or which, in turn, are shared by many Englishes throughout the Anglophone world. Hence, the findings are to be placed within an evolving framework, which takes into account the shifting and dynamic nature of Englishes.

Given the growth of the so-called World Englishes, and the potential influences that they may have on the development of the English language in general, the topics examined in this book appear particularly relevant in gaining new insights into the lexical evolution that the language is undergoing. As will be shown, the creation of a new word is not merely a question of electing a label for a new concept, but labeling such a concept is the first step in the affirmation of the very existence of the concept itself (see Seargeant 2010). Processes related to word formation may assume different configurations in different cultures, and several scholars (see Alabi 2000; Bao 2005; Choi 2006; Adedimeji 2007; Macalister 2007) have focused on their linguistic behavior in cultures where English coexists with other language systems.

The main object of analysis of this book is a selected number of World Englishes, including those which may be more culturally stigmatized. The ultimate aim is not to simply collect descriptions of different English varieties but to investigate them through the use of authentic examples of language in use in order to gain a finer understanding of their lexical peculiarities and make considerations about their development and their reciprocal influences, from a lexical perspective.

Consequently, the theoretical framework goes beyond a purely structuralist approach and tries to include a broader discursive and sociological perspective by focusing on the use of new word formations in authentic situations. The method adopted is fundamentally qualitative; however, some quantitative insights are offered for some of the cases presented with corroborating purposes.

Thus, this volume will serve both as prolegomenon and supplement to other admirable works in the field with the aim of providing an introductory discussion on the theme of word-formation processes in World Englishes, as well as presenting empirical justifications for the observations presented.

Word formation in Englishes is by no means an untilled field. However, the distinctiveness of this book lies in its positioning at the crossroads between studies on varieties of English and on lexicology and, therefore, on a robust interdisciplinary basis. With this consideration, the objective is to go beyond a mere description of the lexical aspects which typify different varieties, and instead to attempt to observe the fluctuant state of English and offer critical reflections which embrace a sociological perspective, rather than adopting a prescriptive or normative standpoint.

1.2 Focus

The desire to concentrate on World Englishes derives from the acknowledgment that the role of these varieties is assuming a growing level of importance for a host of reasons, one of which is the increasing number of speakers. Moreover, although a considerable body of research on Englishes is now available, a discrepancy still exists between the scholarly attention devoted to the so-called standard varieties (see Section 2.4) and other varieties.

The focus of this work is on contemporary varieties. It is certainly true that a language cannot be completely understood without observing its historical developments (for a discussion of the history of English varieties see Momma/Matto 2008), but a diachronic analysis would go beyond the scope of this book. However, some occasional references to specific lexical developments will be made for clarifying purposes.

6   Introduction

This book discusses some thorny issues with no clear-cut solutions. Many a linguist insists on the need to deepen our knowledge of varieties of English which differ (to varying degrees) from the so-called 'native' ones. However, several studies have adopted a rather descriptive approach and, while having the good intentions of shedding a light on lesser-known varieties, have only done so by simply comparing them with the traditional paradigms from which they originally aimed to deviate.

This work avoids entering the debate between, on the one hand, those who apologetically support the necessity of a fixed usage and see linguistic tolerance as a form of linguistic laxism and, on the other hand, those who defend the dynamicity of a language as one of its ineludible characteristics. Rather, it investigates selected English varieties, adopting an exploratory rather than a prescriptive approach. The attempt is to observe how these varieties evolve by analyzing their vocabulary and the main changes that it undergoes. It also describes recent trends in vocabulary developments, as well as the formation of neologisms and the reciprocal lexical influences emerging across varieties.

The analysis will be limited to a restricted number of varieties. Indeed, given the complexity of the notion of World Englishes, the inescapable contaminations among different Englishes, and the dynamicity of the language, it is deemed impossible to offer a comprehensive overview of all contemporary varieties. Without abstaining completely from references to the historical, phonetic and phonological, syntactical, textual, and pragmatic aspects, as are deemed critical to understanding fully the peculiarities of a certain variety, the focus is on the lexicon of different Englishes in the world. The need to adopt a lexical approach springs from the idea that the understanding of the vocabulary is decisive for the study of a certain language variety. Thus, lexical formations are used as a lens for observing the multitude of Englishes and their dynamic usages.

The selection is conducted according to given parameters such as the (necessarily approximate) number of speakers or the socio-cultural importance attributed to such varieties, without disregarding the flexibility and the subjectivity which are inherent in these parameters. Moreover, the level of standardization is also taken into account. This is not to say that only highly standardized varieties are considered relevant, but simply that the analysis will acknowledge their level of standardization and codification.

The concept of codification has been described *inter alia* by Schneider (2007), who offers an investigation into the codification of postcolonial varieties, and Tieken-Bonn van Ostade (2012), who focuses on the developments of the same process in England. For the purpose of this book, it is critical to highlight that codification can follow prescriptive or descriptive patterns. The former case presupposes the existence of rules which are specifically laid down at a theoretical level. Conversely, in the latter case, rules generally describe how the language is used in practice. Following well-established contemporary trends, the focus of this book is on critical description. The aim is not to see whether a variety complies, or not, with a predetermined set of rules, but to observe different forms of language in use or discourses. On a practical note, codification is often associated with grammar, spelling, punctuation, and, at times, pronunciation. However, vocabulary is also subject to such processes and represents the focus of this study.

Lexicography has been defined as the "first arm" of codification (Kachru 2005: 224) and, indeed, lexicographic resources play a significant role in the codification process of a language. In this respect, Schneider (2007: 52) talks about a "mutually reinforcing process", in which "new national identities cause an awareness of the existence of new language varieties, which in turn causes the production of dictionaries of these new varieties; once such a dictionary is out it strengthens the distinct national and linguistic identity". Clearly, the mere existence of a dictionary of a specific variety does not necessarily determine its wide sociolinguistic acceptance.

Codification and standardization may therefore appear as fragmented and inconsistent phenomena, whose description inevitably assumes an ephemeral and transient meaning, if not an unattainable one. However, these processes are interpreted in this work as fundamental and inherent in language development. Noticeably, the level of diversification, in terms of, among others, geographical and sociological contexts, types of users, and scope, makes it essential to reflect upon the impossibility of capturing a fixed standard and describing it in definite terms. This diversification inexorably generates the need for ontologies which may successfully represent the fluidity and flexibility of English varieties and which confirm the basic assumption that English is to be investigated as a language compound rather than as a mythical monolithic entity.

1.3 Structure of the book

This book is divided into three main parts. Part 1 is preparatory and introduces the conceptual underpinnings of this work. It also presents the rationale for the approach chosen. Part 2 sketches some of the definitional problems surrounding word-formation phenomena and describes the methodological framework applied. Part 3 is of an analytical nature; it presents selected cases, and subsequently offers some concluding remarks.

8 *Introduction*

Chapter 1 illustrates the pivotal aims of the work and the research gap which the analysis aims to fill. It also offers preliminary explanations regarding the choice made to focus exclusively on lexical aspects.

Chapter 2 presents the genesis of the World Englishes model and discusses the theoretical background adopted for the investigation of neologisms and word-formation processes. More specifically, it describes the evolutionary processes of World Englishes and introduces the need to rethink traditional paradigms due to the complexity and the dynamicity which characterize varieties of English across the globe, as well as the necessity of keeping abreast of changing parameters when presenting a framework. It discusses complex issues related to the categorization of different varieties of English, presenting some of the available models from a critical perspective. It also deals with other crucial notions such as nativeness and standardization in language, which have maintained a persistent foothold in the field. In particular, it offers an introduction to the concept of nativeness and provides an overview of the different perspectives which determine its predominant contemporary interpretations.

Chapter 3 focuses on themes of productivity and creativity in the English language. Subsequently, it delves more precisely into the world of neologisms and presents some of the theories which have been suggested when describing the same. Finally, it offers a critical discussion of the evolution of neologisms as deriving from nonce-formation.

Chapter 4 provides a systematic description of the most frequent word-formation processes which may be adopted in the creation of a neologism. It topicalizes some important notions in the fields of lexicology and morphology and applies them in order to lay out a typology of the processes emerging in World Englishes. It also stresses the idea that some of these dynamics may assume blurred contours, by providing a critical investigation of the different classifications of word-formation phenomena offered in the literature.[1]

Chapter 5 describes some of the most influential methodological frameworks suitable for the investigation of neologisms. It briefly introduces the corpora which provide data for the analyses conducted in Chapter 6, and it describes the research approach adopted in the analytical section.

Chapter 6 presents eight case studies which focus on the emergence of neologisms in different varieties. Given the number of varieties and dialects of English spoken around the world, a detailed description of all of them would be an unachievable task, especially taking into consideration that, within a single variety of English, significant peculiarities are displayed by specific communities of practice or even at an individual level.

The conclusion places the findings of the book within the current debate on World Englishes. It discusses the issue of deriving irrefutable generalizations from context-specific data, but also summarizes the insights offered by the analysis in order to show how lexical investigation can be indicative of specific cultural and linguistic mutations at an inter-varietal or intra-varietal level. It concludes that the notion of World Englishes has to be rekindled unceasingly for the paradigm to continue to adapt to new sociolinguistic situations.

Note

1 This chapter is functional to the full appreciation of Chapter 6 in which these processes are examined in relation to different varieties of English across the globe.

2 Investigating English and Englishes

At a conference in Verona some years ago,[1] David Crystal semi-seriously reminded us that we should never trust anyone who presents statistics on the number of English speakers in the world. Indeed, the problematization of who should be counted as a speaker of a given language has long been the object of extensive scholarly research (Graddol 2006).

Firstly, the unimaginable difficulty inherent in providing such statistics is explained by practical contingencies, such as the fact that precise and updated census data are not always accessible. This is particularly the case with English, as it has assumed the function of a global language, with figures varying significantly. In particular, the number of English speakers in populous countries such as China, where the statistics presented often show noticeable discrepancies, has a significant impact on the magnitude of these differences (Bolton/Graddol 2012). Also critical are the theoretical issues in establishing the criteria by which a speaker of a language should be defined as one. Elements such as the geographic area or the level of proficiency cannot provide a solid basis for calculating the number of English speakers in any incontrovertible way, considering that these factors inevitably assume arbitrary and elusive contours. The impossibility of providing definite data is also linked to the notion of English itself, which is multifaceted and debated.

In this respect, the expression 'English language complex' suggested by McArthur (2003: 56) captures the many-sided and unique nature of contemporary English. Similarly, the label 'English compound' will be used here to show the multiple, and at the same time single/singular, nature of English and its varieties.

Without entering into an ontological discussion of the nature of the English language, this chapter presents some considerations on the most influential interpretative models which have been adopted to describe it and its varieties in recent years. Far from being a comprehensive review, it offers some guidelines to frame the role and development of English internationally, which in turn provides the basis for a fuller understanding of the lexical developments that varieties of English undergo around the globe.

World Englishes are investigated especially with regard to their lexical peculiarities and their ability to influence even mainstream forms of English from this perspective. The ultimate objective is to observe word-formation processes in a series of varieties in order to investigate lexical innovation and linguistic changes (also as potential epitomes of cultural variations) in English around the world.

2.1 Definitional issues

A wide range of terminological choices to refer to different varieties of English may be adopted. For instance, the expression 'New Englishes' (see Pride 1982; Biermeier 2008) emphasizes their chronological aspect (see Section 1.1). New Englishes have been defined as "recently emerging and increasingly autonomous variet[ies] of English, especially in a non-western setting, such as India, Nigeria, or Singapore" (McArthur 1992: 688). However, Kachru (1983) stressed early on the questionability of the very idea of 'new' in that, for example, the 'New English' spoken in India is actually older than others which are not generally considered as new, such as that spoken in Australia. Moreover, the notion of New Englishes has now been in use for several decades to denote a series of varieties which were not originally contemplated as standard. However, the concept of standard itself is highly problematic (see Section 2.4), and it is not always clear whether forms of English, such as English as a Lingua Franca (ELF), should be ascribed to the category of New Englishes.

The chronological criterion is not the only one adopted in this study and some varieties which have not developed 'recently', e.g. the above-cited Indian one(s), are discussed, given their importance as regards the number of speakers, their sociological status, or their political impact.

Definitional choices are often based on historical processes, as happens in the case of 'Postcolonial English' (e.g. Schneider 2007). In this view, it is evident that some of the English varieties have developed in postcolonial contexts but, given the complexity of the relationships between different standards of English, they cannot be understood simply as an outcome of British imperialism. Rather, they may be seen as a consequence of intricate globalization phenomena. On a practical note, it should be pointed out that the focus of this book is mainly synchronic and is not theoretically limited to varieties which have developed in the postcolonial era.

The expression 'lesser-known varieties' (Schreier et al. 2010) may also be applied to describe a specific set of Englishes, but it will not be employed in this work. Indeed, the forms of English discussed do not comply with all the criteria illustrated by Schreier et al. (2010: 4) to define lesser-known forms of English, namely:

1. Usage as FL and not as English as a Second Language (ESL) or English as a Foreign Language (EFL)
2. Identification as a distinctive variety
3. "Associated with stable communities or regions"
4. Spoken by minority groups
5. Often "originally transmitted by settler communities"
6. "Formed by processes of dialect and/or language contact"
7. Functioning as "identity carriers"
8. "Often endangered".

In particular, the first factor listed does not commonly apply to the varieties observed in this book, as in many of the geographical areas investigated English may be used as a form of ESL or EFL (e.g. in India). The identification as a distinctive variety (be it a type of intra-communitarian or extra-communitarian identification) characterizes most of the forms of English presented here. However, as they often develop along a continuum, it may be debatable whether a certain variety should be equated to an autonomous language or not. Therefore, choosing which form to investigate (whether basilectal, mesolectal, or acrolectal) may also be problematic. Although in certain communities specific movements may favor the use of other local languages, the growth of English is manifest in several societies. In this regard, the role of English as an identity carrier is controversial. Indeed, a certain tension often exists between the use of English as a necessity and that of other local languages as the expression of an identity trait, especially in those countries where English is used as ESL or EFL. On a final note, the varieties analyzed are generally neither spoken by minorities nor officially considered to be endangered.

In light of the complexity and the heterogeneity of the sociolinguistic contexts in which English is employed, Adedimeji stresses the global and, at the same time, local nature of the Englishes spoken in the world: "English is now seen as a global language, susceptible to the subtleties and idiosyncrasies of regional and cultural linguistic behaviours" (Adedimeji 2007: 2).

This tension may be summarized in the notion of 'glocalized' forms of English (Pakir 1999), where Glocal English refers to a language which is global and yet deeply rooted in the local contexts. Thus, it has international status in its global spread, but at the same time expresses local identities. In this respect, it should be pointed out that a global language will never equate to a global culture (Ke 2015), even though the level of intelligibilty among people is constantly increasing. Indeed, as Ke (2015) aptly remarks, linguistic, cultural, political, and social differences will always characterize modern societies and this is reflected in the fluidity and the dynamicity of global English.

The term Word Englishes is deemed relatively neutral and at the same time apt to emphasize the immense geographical expansion that English in its different forms has reached. The approaches which may be subsumed under the expression World Englishes are very diverse as regards their linguistic and philosophical fundaments. This work predominantly makes use of the expression World Englishes (also following *inter alia* Kachru 1985, 1997) intended to include the different varieties of English which may be found across the globe. Although apparently tautological, this definition allows us to adopt an inclusive, rather than exclusive, perspective and to acknowledge the international character of the English language as well as its plural nature. There is also the awareness that no model can represent an exhaustive picture of all varieties and frame them squarely into precise categories.

More specifically, this expression is to be distinguished from World English in its singular form, intended as an international language which acts as a common means of communication, sharing similarities across the globe despite geographical distances. Along the same lines, other expressions such as 'World International English' (WIE) or 'World Standard English' (WSE) have been coined. Although seemingly paradoxical, in that it refers to a unique language and at the same time to an incredibly vast compound of languages, WSE describes "an evolving 'super-standard' that is comfortable with both territorial and linguistic diversity" (McArthur 2002: 448).

This concept is somehow in accordance with the notion of English as a Lingua Franca (see House 1999, *inter alia*), although, at least in its more restrictive interpretation, ELF refers specifically to a language used by people whose native language is not English. It should not be based on any specific national standard, but be seen as a separate and multifaceted entity, with its own ontologies and, at the same time, as the expression of heterogeneous tendencies. Thus, it is clear that the form of English spoken by a vast number of speakers in the world is in line with the features of ELF (see Seidlhofer 2011) which, given the vastness of its use, simply cannot be labeled as a simplified, improper form of English. Even though this work does not have ELF as a focal point, it is evident that its developments have, and will continue to have, a noteworthy influence on English and its characteristics. Indeed, although the phenomenon of a lingua franca is not new (see European Commission 2011), globalization processes have increased and hastened the need for a supranational language with a predominately communicative purpose.

2.2 Categorizations and their limitations

Several models have been developed in recent decades in order to provide a visual representation of English and its varieties in the world. Without aiming to offer an exhaustive overview, some of the most influential models will now be discussed in an attempt to contribute critical reflections on selected classifications by showing their significance and their limitations.[2] In this respect, as early as 1992, McArthur noted:

> The first truism is that the day-to-day language acts of users of English worldwide – thought, spoken, written, typed, printed, broadcast, taped, telephoned, faxed, and emailed – are so vast that no person, group, or system could ever catch and catalogue them all.
>
> (McArthur 1992: 78)

Indeed, no model or categorization can fully represent the complexity of English, its dynamic and kaleidoscopic nature, and the infinite nuances which characterize its varieties. As Onysko notes (2016), the human tendency to categorize items is innate, but categorizations may be inadequate to depict intricate phenomena.

The 'World System of Englishes' (Mair 2013) model has been adopted as an analytical framework aiming to show hierarchies which may be unexpected (Mair 2014) in light of globalization and mediatization dynamics. More specifically, Mair (2013, 2014), drawing on de Swaan (2013/2002), develops a model based on the World System of Standard and Non-standard Englishes, which is hierarchically divided into distinct categories, as illustrated in Table 2.1 (adapted from Mair 2013: 264; Mair 2014).

The hierarchical power that certain varieties assume cannot be disregarded. At the same time, however, this model does not offer a problematization of the fluidity of the concept of standard. Moreover, it does not seem to adequately emphasize that varietal boundaries are often porous and unstable. As a necessary shortcoming, this typology does not clearly conceive potential shifts from one category to another over time. Furthermore, defining Standard American English as the only hyper-central variety calls for a deeper reflection on the Americanization of English. Indeed, although such a process is undeniably taking place, establishing the existence of a sole 'hub' of English in the world appears to some extent an oversimplification.

Another influential model adopted to describe the evolution of English varieties is the Dynamic Model of Postcolonial Englishes (PCE) (Schneider 2003, 2007), which is based on the assumption that "there is an underlying uniform process which has driven the individual historical instantiations of PCEs growing in different localities" (Schneider 2007: 21).

Table 2.1 World System of Standard and Non-standard Englishes

Categories
A hyper-central variety / hub of the World System of Englishes: Standard American English

B super-central varieties:
   (1) standard:
     British English, Australian English, South African English, Nigerian English, Indian English, and a very small number of others
   (2) non-standard:
     African-American Vernacular English, Jamaican Creole, popular London, and a very small number of others
     (+ domain-specific ELF uses: science, business, international law, etc.)

C central varieties:
   (1) standard:
     Irish English, Scottish (Standard) English, Jamaican English, Ghanaian English, Kenyan English, Sri Lankan English, Pakistani English, New Zealand English, and a small number of others
   (2) non-standard:
     Northern English urban koinés, US Southern, and a small number of others

D peripheral varieties

This model suggests that emerging varieties undergo five consecutive stages, namely Foundation; Exonormative Stabilization; Nativization; Endonormative Stabilization; and Differentiation. Such stages are outlined below:

1. *Foundation*: English is established in a new area, usually as a result of colonial expansion.
2. *Exonormative Stabilization*: After political stabilization, contacts between settlers and local population increase.
3. *Nativization*: Cultural and linguistic transformations take place, with the emergence of structures which are distinctive to the new variety. A study on World Englishes inevitably has to take into account Kachru's idea of 'nativization' (Kachru 1981), which implies systematic changes of linguistic features deriving from the use of English in new sociocultural contexts. In a similar vein, McArthur (1992) defines 'nativation' as follows: "the process by which a transplanted language becomes native to a people or place, either in addition to or in place of any language or languages already in use. The process is often given a specific name, such as Africanization or Indianization (in the case of English), and takes place at every level of language" (McArthur 1992: 682–683).

4   *Endonormative Stabilization*: It culminates in the identity separation of the local variety and its codification, as well as lexical creativity.
5   *Differentiation*: Internal differentiation increases with the emergence of new sociolects within the variety (Schneider 2014).

Along these lines, I would like to suggest that differentiation could potentially be followed by subsequent phases. Indeed, after the differentiation process there may be tendencies towards reciprocal influences, and this phase may be defined as cross-fertilization. The empirical testing of this thesis goes beyond the scope of this book, but it represents a further potential avenue for research in the field of Postcolonial Englishes.

Whether the PCE model is also applicable *tout court* to all World Englishes in contemporary contexts remains open to debate. In this respect, Schneider's (2014) update focuses on the development of transnational attraction dynamics, and the author himself points out that "the Dynamic Model is not really, or only to a rather limited extent, a suitable framework to describe this new kind of dynamism of global Englishes" (Schneider 2014: 27–28).

Some integrative agendas which recontextualize the dynamic model have also been suggested, for example by Buschfeld and Kautzsch (2017) with their Extra- and Intra-territorial Forces (EIF) framework.

This model is based on the notion of extra-territorial and intra-territorial forces, which may be summarized in the following categories (Buschfeld/Kautzsch 2017: 106):

A   Extra-territorial forces:

- colonization
- language policies
- globalization
- foreign policies
- sociodemographic background.

B   Intra-territorial forces:

- attitudes towards colonization
- language policies / language attitudes
- 'acceptance' of globalization
- foreign policies
- sociodemographic background.

This model aims at an integrative classification of PCEs and non-PCEs as well as ESL and EFL varieties. The attempt is to portray these different forms of English through the lens of the above-mentioned forces and in light of their diachronic evolution.

As mentioned above, Kachru's (1985) seminal model has long been used to broadly depict English varieties in the world, which may be categorized into three concentric circles: inner, outer and expanding. They are traditionally seen as broadly corresponding to English as a Native Language (ENL), ESL and ELF varieties, as noted by Schneider (2003: 237).[3] According to this view, countries such as the United Kingdom, the United States, Australia, Canada, and New Zealand belong to the inner circle, while the outer circle includes countries (often former colonies) where English has an official or semi-official status, such as Nigeria, India, Malaysia, and the Philippines. Finally, the expanding circle consists of all countries where English is used as a foreign language, thus ranging from Japan to Brazil, and from Italy to China.

In has often been pointed out that the original model shows some deficiencies (Bruthiaux 2003: 161–171; Jenkins 2003: 17–18). Indeed, this ontology seems to some extent incompatible with contemporary paradigms of World Englishes, which account for the complex network of (intertwined) varieties and imply a theoretically egalitarian status of all Englishes. More precisely, the main limitations of the original Kachruvian model may be summarized as follows:

1. Lack of problematization of native/non-native (see Bonfiglio 2007 on the deconstruction of notions such as native and mother tongue).
2. No clear definition of the elements categorized, as there is a broad reference to nations, types of speakers, and functions of English, as well as its varieties, which leads to the obfuscation of sociolinguistic complexities (Bruthiaux 2003). In particular, no emphasis is placed on the specific pragmatic functions that the English language assumes in certain contexts and within specific communities of practice.
3. Exclusive use of the geographical criterion. This aspect is not sufficient in that it disregards considerable variations within each circle, and even within each of the countries cited as examples.
4. Lack of adequate dynamicity. Although not completely static, the model fails to emphasize the dynamicity inherent in language use and it ultimately places language speakers within fixed and immovable categories.
5. Impenetrability of the circles. Intuitively, all circles are interconnected, but the fluidity which exists between circles is not clearly contemplated. Kachru (1997) himself highlights that the model is an oversimplification, but it should be emphasized that the categories are not mutually exclusive and are also highly interconnected and interdependent.

Moreover, the model does not include the concept of English as a Lingua Franca as a variety of the expanding circle, as suggested by Mollin (2006). Indeed, if we adopt the notion of ELF as a "variety of English" (Mauranen 2003: 514), it could be argued that, if intended in its purest form, ELF ought to be positioned within the expanding circle. However, it has also been stated that the concept of ELF somehow transcends this model in that ELF interactions concern not only the expanding circle but also the outer and the inner ones and transversally involve all speakers of English (Seidlhofer 2011).

The tripartite model has also been criticized for not capturing all the multifarious nuances, and the vast number of different linguistic situations, in countries where English is spoken in some form, especially given the complexification of language identities. The inner circle has traditionally been assigned a normative role, being regarded as pure and correct. However, even within countries of the inner circle, the situation is often highly heterogeneous. Indeed, even where English is the only official language, other tongues may be used (for example, due to the constant movement of people). The outer circle undergoes complex endonormative processes, with the codification and the standardization of specific English varieties, which are not simply aiming at replicating or imitating inner ones but are, instead, an expression of a specific local linguistic and cultural identity. Moreover, the Englishes spoken in the expanding circle are no longer considered as necessarily inadequate in relation to the other varieties but are constantly acquiring an independent and recognized status.

In other words, in its original form the inner circle is commonly seen as endonormative, while the expanding circle as exonormative, thus meaning that norms are imposed from the outside and implying an automatic application of the norms of one variety to another. However, it is clear that, even in the expanding circle, normative standards are endogenously created, and it is also even possible that the norms of native varieties are influenced by external ones (see Crystal 2003).

Despite the limitations inherent in any model attempting to depict a multifaceted linguistic situation, Kachru's representation remains remarkably valuable in that it aims at considering (potentially) a vast number of varieties and goes beyond the traditional paradigm which described English exclusively as the language of its native speakers. Indeed, although apparently native-centered, the model actually stresses that English displays "multicultural identities" (Kachru 1992: 357) and does not conceptualize English as the expression of a monolithic language belonging solely to natives, identified as such through preconceived criteria.

Moreover, the Kachruvian concept of World Englishes (WE) was groundbreaking especially with regard to the inclusive conceptualization of 'WE-ness':

Investigating English and Englishes 19

This concept emphasizes "WE-ness", and not the dichotomy between *us* and *them* (the native and non-native users). In this sense, then, English is a valuable linguistic tool used for various functions. The approaches to the study of world Englishes, therefore, have to be interdisciplinary and integrative, and different methodologies must be used (literary, linguistic, and pedagogical) to capture distinct identities of different Englishes, and to examine critically the implications of such identities in cross-cultural communication and creativity.

(Kachru 1997: 212).

These words encapsulate the awareness that traditional dichotomic paradigms fail to acknowledge the sociolinguistic complexity of the contexts in which English is used.

In this respect, Bolton (2005: 75) stresses that "the Kachruvian model of the three circles was never intended to be monolithic and unchanging". In particular, Kachru's 1997 discussion of the Circles of English (see Kachru 1997: 213) emphasizes the potential overlaps between circles, although this aspect remains to some extent inchoate. It should also be noted that the homogenization of categories inevitably impedes capturing the deep differences, and also the nuances, which typify a variety. Indeed, no two countries within a circle are the same, and no one country has a linguistic situation which is completely unproblematic and uniform from a classificatory viewpoint.

From a related but different perspective, McArthur (1999) talks about the need to investigate English from at least three different standpoints, given that the characteristics and functions of various forms of English may vary considerably. More specifically, he discusses the global, continental/regional, and national/local level (1999: 1), as outlined in Figure 2.1.

Different forms of English operate in specific circumstances and settings. They are not mutually exclusive and, to some extent, their coexistence in

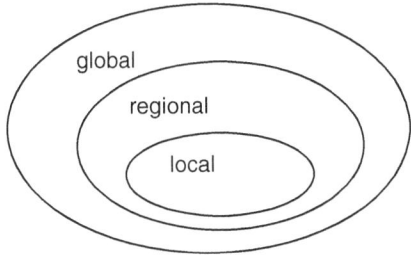

Figure 2.1 Levels of English in the world (adapted from McArthur 1999)

given contexts is in line with the phenomenon of multiglossia. Indeed, the heterogeneity and complexity of the speech repertoires which certain communities display may determine the presence of a variegated continuum of local, regional and global varieties.

With the attempt to go beyond the impenetrability of distinct circles, Graddol (1997) suggests a model (to some extent drawing on Kachru's seminal representation) in which some degree of contamination between the categories is envisaged, thanks to the use of arrows which connect one circle to the next. However, if this ontology is adopted, it is equally important to underline that the contaminating stimulus is not unidirectional but takes place at all levels.

In this respect, Figure 2.2 draws on the basic representation of Graddol's model but has been adapted with the intention of predominantly illustrating the fluidity which exists between the different circles (visually represented by the use of dotted lines), as well as their reciprocal influences (pictorially indicated with bidirectional arrows).

This visualization implies that inner varieties are not assigned the exclusive prerogative to influence others, but the process is fluid and circular. Moreover, it aims to depict the porousness of the different circles.

Following Bruthiaux (2003), some criteria should be adopted for the conceptualization of a model. For example, equilibrium between accuracy in terms of sociolinguistic description and clarity of presentation should be sought. This may lead to an apparent simplification, but one that is necessary in order to preserve the explanatory intelligibility intrinsic in a successful model.

Any model aiming at representing contemporary English varieties should take into account the notion of pluricentrism. The idea of English linguistic pluricentrism is well established (see Leitner 1992) and may be seen as an acknowledgment of (and a reaction to) the constant complexification of the status of English usage in the world. It abandons the idea of a monolithic entity to be adopted as a reference model and supports the assumption that several varieties may be considered as standards. Emphasis, therefore, is

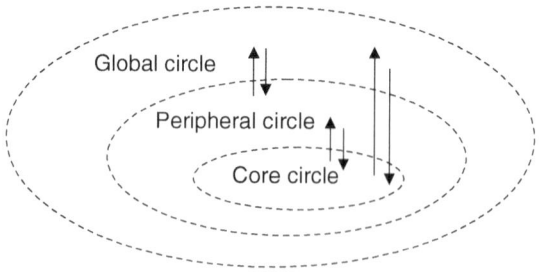

Figure 2.2 Englishes and their permeability

Investigating English and Englishes 21

not placed on nativeness but on the combination of other language factors. On a practical note, in the following chapters, references to the concept of native and non-native speakers will sometimes be used in line with a certain terminological tradition simply for the sake of conciseness. It is, however, essential that the roles of speakers, and their categorization in terms of nativeness, be highly problematized as they cannot be assigned on an *a priori* basis (see Section 2.3).

This work stresses the merit of adopting a pluricentric perspective rather than focusing on a purely geographical division, in that a model which takes into account multiple parameters appears more adequate in depicting the complexity of English varieties. Some of these parameters are:

- proficiency
- intelligibility with other varieties
- number of speakers.

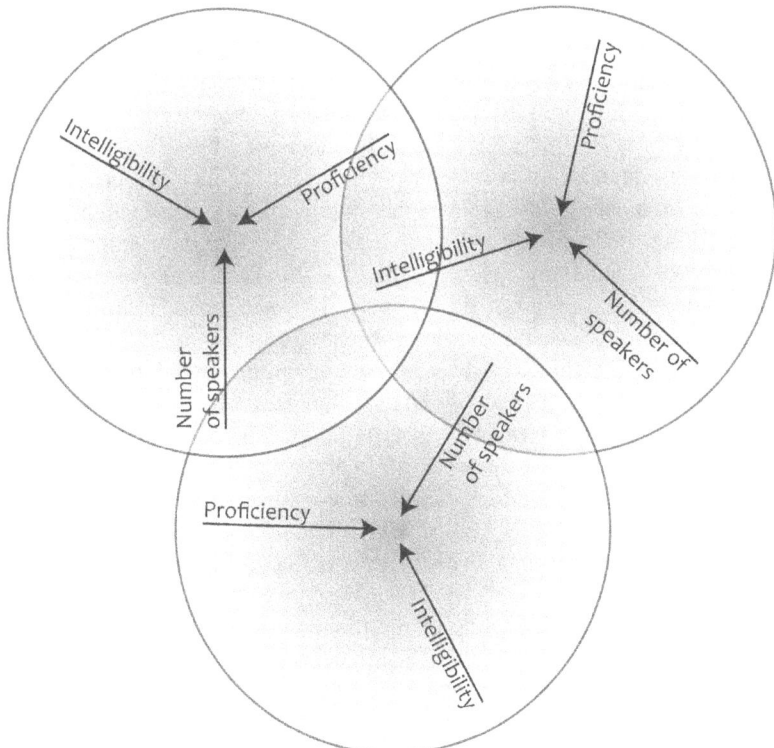

Figure 2.3 English transnational polycentrism

Figure 2.3 attempts to illustrate a polycentric conception of English varieties. Its scope is not to present all the possible factors involved, but to observe how contemporary English is a transnational being which cannot automatically be equated to one single core. Beyond its heuristic value, such a representation allows us to pinpoint some specific elements which may contribute to the diffusion of a certain variety.

Of the many models available, no pictorial reproduction seems completely satisfactory to adequately stress the cross-fertilization process that the English compound undergoes in all its forms. Indeed, despite the illustrative power that they possess, such models inevitably tend to represent varieties of English[4] as single, independent entities, which can of course have diverse levels of relatedness but are still inherently understood as profoundly self-standing.

As mentioned above, in any model-making procedure a balance has to be found between a finely drawn illustration and a general depiction of a phenomenon. Consequently, the visualization suggested in Figure 2.3 is inevitably criticizable, for instance as regards the complexities inherent in the attempt to define intelligibility. In their influential work, Munro and Derwing (1995) conceptualize intelligibility as a basis for pronunciation pedagogy and conceive it in relation to comprehensibility and accentedness. Intelligibility is operationalized as "the extent to which the speaker's intended utterance is actually understood by a listener" (1995: 291). Subsequently, in his Centripetal Circles Model of International English, Modiano (1999) assumes that intelligibility is self-evident to language users. In this regard, Jenkins (2003) questions how intelligibility may be described and measured, according to whom, and to which paradigms, and also highlights the role played by accommodation practices. It can also be argued that intelligibility may somehow be included under the label of proficiency. However, despite its limitation and instability, the concept of intelligibility assumes an important (and of course multifaceted) function, not only in terms of language knowledge and competence, but also from a sociolinguistic perspective in that it may fruitfully be employed to investigate the perception of interlocutor diversity. It should also be pointed out that a form of English which is not intelligible to others may also encounter problems in its diffusion and recognition as a variety of the English language.

Despite its limitations, one of the main functions of the polycentric model is that of moving beyond a monocentric conception of English, rather than aspiring to be comprehensive and all-inclusive in depicting the multifaceted nature of the English compound. In this model, factors such as the level of proficiency, rather than geographical elements, are assigned prominence and are used to represent the community of English speakers (see Graddol 2006). Indeed, the identification of a country does not necessarily correspond to a specific level of language proficiency. For instance, the USA is part of the inner circle, but for some citizens English is not a native language, and it is estimated that approximately 40 million people speak Spanish as their first language. The number of speakers using a certain variety is a crucial datum to take into consideration, as the users of a language inevitably shape the language itself, in line with the now axiomatic principle that English changes according to its users.

2.3 Nativeness

The category of nativeness is not self-explanatory, especially as regards the multifaceted sphere of English where infinite levels of proficiency and contexts of usages are found. Indeed, the nativeness paradigm has often been criticized because it is founded on a binary taxonomy (natives vs nonnatives), which seems to admit the existence of self-defining categories and to disregard the complexity of any linguistic situation. Consequently, this facile distinction brings with it intricate issues.

Although nativeness is, in turn, considered to be a fundamental or a mythic subject in linguistics (Rajagopalan 1997: 226; see also Davies 2003), the question regarding who can be defined as a native speaker of a given tongue has been topical in language studies. Native varieties were long considered as the sole legitimate model to be adopted for language description and teaching purposes, but questions related to who may ultimately be assigned the role of custodian of the adequacy of performance remain open to debate.

Some people strongly assume that the concept of nativeness is self-defined and indisputable. Conversely, others label nativeness as a 'myth', as does Ferguson who radically defines the constructs of native speaker and mother tongue as mystical and argues for their dismissal from any linguist's agenda (Ferguson 1983).

The interpretation of nativeness as a monolithic construct is fraught with fallacious presuppositions, as many a scholar has pointed out in past decades. For instance, Mesthrie (2006: 386–387) purports that English has always developed within a multilingual context, with Celtic and Scandinavian languages, Latin, and Norman French being some of the ones which have, in different manners and to varying degrees, coexisted with some form of English across the centuries.

Thus, the idea of a pure and untouched English language belonging to speakers who can unproblematically be defined as native speakers seems an idealized vision of what has always been a much more convoluted phenomenon. Without suggesting the demise of the concept of nativeness, its problematization is put forward especially in line with Singh's (1998) observation that nativeness is generally conceived in terms of monolingualism, although we are actually living in the era of multilingualism. Moreover, in many countries, varied repertoires of Englishes clearly exist. In this view, I concur with Brutt-Griffler and Samimy when they state that "the more English becomes an international language, the more the division of its speakers into 'native' and 'nonnative' becomes inconsistent" (Brutt-Griffler/Samimy 2001: 105).

Following the traditional paradigm, nativeness is related to early acquisition and authority in judgment (see McArthur 1992: 682), as well as level of performance and acceptance within a certain community of speakers. However, no structural criterion appears sufficient to set clear boundaries between natives and non-natives, and the instability and heterogeneity of such categories is manifest. More specifically, many questions have been raised regarding the possibility of applying fixed measures for definitional purposes in the case of nativeness. These are, for instance: whether early acquisition means exclusively from birth or can be extended to a later age; whether linguistically impaired people may still be assigned a level of performance definable as native; whether emigration can alter the status of native; whether a low level of performance in terms of grammatical or lexical accuracy determined by a very young age or by poor education may affect the native paradigm, and so on (see Hackert 2012: 13–14). Consequently, traditional definitions of nativeness seem pseudo-procedural in that they are inevitably ideologically laden and normatively derived.

No decisive conclusions can be made about the nature of native varieties vis-à-vis their non-native counterparts. The major problem pertains to the inevitable overlap between the two categories and the criteria employed when ascribing a variety to the former or latter group. Indeed, typological descriptions (which are often tentative and inexorably incomplete and unstable) are clearly insufficient to provide a radical distinction.

Nativeness may be seen as a "non-elective socially constructed identity rather than a linguistic category" (Brutt-Griffler/Samimy 2001: 100). Thus, the social aspects which contribute to the definition of nativeness cannot be disregarded. Davies (2003) also examines the manifold relationship between the definition of natives and ideological constructs, and shows that individual and societal aspects of nativeness are in constant flux. Along these lines, rather than focusing exclusively on psycholinguistic aspects, a lengthy strand of research has acknowledged the cultural and political nature of nativeness. This study also aims to emphasize the socio-culturally anchored essence of this concept.

Studies based on contrastive analyses between native and second-language varieties are innumerable (e.g. Görlach 1995: 79). However, although this type of comparison is sometimes essential in order to identify the peculiarities of a certain variety, one of the overarching principles of this work is that all varieties should be considered as autonomous, albeit constantly cross-contaminating systems, and should not necessarily be observed as insufficient or inadequate in comparison to any of the 'core varieties'. This approach derives from the acknowledgment that new imperatives of communication have determined an evolution of the relationships between different varieties, which are constantly shifting from a stable, hierarchical, monocentric conception to a dynamic, hybrid, and polycentric one.

2.4 Standard(s) in language

The notion of standard has been center stage in several language studies (e.g. Mugglestone 2007/1995; Lippi-Green 2011/1997; Hickey 2012 to name but a few), and it has inspired the emergence of conspicuous research which has maintained a pervasive purchase in linguistics. However, it has become so much a part of the field that its theoretical foundations are not often overtly focused on. The standard construct has proven durable because it allows for a binary distinction between standard and non-standard, but these categories are often employed without a constant definition and redefinition, as would be required by a scientific approach.

A standard may be described as following three main criteria in general, which do not necessarily coexist, especially if we consider the language situation in the Web 2.0 era:

1 Social status: a standard is mostly regarded as a prestigious variety. It lacks stigmatization (by most speakers) and is often spoken by educated people.
2 Prescriptive nature: it is used in lexicographic resources and manuals and is often taught in schools as a reference model. Nevertheless, teaching and training materials show a growing awareness of the importance of representing the heterogeneity of every language.
3 Diffuse usage: it is customarily linked to the language employed in traditional media, which are considered particularly influential in terms of standardization processes. However, the pluralization of media has also brought with it a considerable differentiation from a linguistic perspective.

A standard language is, to a large extent, an idealized and ideological construct, which often leads to the stigmatization of varieties which are considerably different. Coupland and Jaworski (2004: 36) highlight that "language is necessarily used against background sets of assumptions" and these assumptions are inevitably ideological. Therefore, one may ask: what level of linguistic variation should be tolerated to say that a certain variety is standard? In addition, how should such variation be evaluated, and according to what prototypical form of language?

2.4.1 English standards

The concept of standard in languages is remarkably multifarious and, especially in the case of English, protean and elusive. In his controversial book on Standard English, Honey (1997) remarks that changes need to be approved by the educated community in order to be accepted, and the criterion of acceptability is strictly related to the notion of authority (1997: 147). Conversely, starting from a completely different theoretical background and going beyond Honey's prescriptive approach,[5] Milroy (2002) affirms that a standard is related to the idea of "high status" but also stresses that "it is the high status of speakers that is involved, not of language, since language in its internal properties is indifferent to status" (Milroy 2002: 23). Thus, the notions of education and 'educatedness' inevitably play a role, but the concept of Standard English cannot be seen as self-explanatory, nor as superior to other varieties according to any purely linguistic criteria.

Hickey defines Standard English as a "supranational form of written English which is normally used in printing, in various documents of an official nature and which is taught to foreigners" and adds that "spoken standard English is not a single form of the language but is represented by the supraregional varieties in different Anglophone countries" (Hickey 2004: 668). However, it should also be pointed out that a neat distinction between spoken and written forms of English seems to disregard the complexity and hybridity that certain modes may display, especially in the digital era.

Traditionally, the existence of a simplistic model such as that of Standard English has long been accepted, even though it has often been defined essentially as a myth (Lippi-Green 2011/1997). However, it should be noted that, although it may not be found in everyday situations, its theorization, and the attempt to apply and promote it, have real and tangible effects in terms of language teaching, policing, and socio-cultural stereotypes.

The need to theorize a standard of English is often linked to a fear of the jeopardization of reference models and of the so-called "Babelization" (McArthur 1994: 233) of English. More specifically, in some cases the problematization of the notion of standard has been interpreted as the promotion of an anti-standard ethos which may cause a diaspora of English and its development into unintelligible languages. However, the contemporary socio-political situation is radically different from that which caused the diaspora of languages in previous centuries and, thus, this fear appears unfounded (Quirk 2014: 5). In this respect, many applaud McKay's view, which discusses the speculative and visionary nature of the presumed risk of such a development:

> It is puzzling that whereas differences in the use of English between Inner Circle countries are generally accepted, with no one suggesting that this will lead to incomprehensibility, language variation outside Inner Circle countries is often seen as a threat.
> (McKay 2002: 49–50)

The concept of an anti-standard ethos plays a crucial role in understanding the development of English, as it is linked to a certain level of reluctance by some communities of speakers to adjust to a predetermined standard, which could be seen as unnatural or detrimental to the enhancement of their own identity and culture.

The expression 'standards of English' (Hickey 2012) in a plural form seems to capture the multitude of standards available in a more coherent way, without espousing a monocentric view which sees a superior variety as the only model to be adopted. As Hickey (2012: 1) notes, "a pluralistic conception of standard English is thus likely to be closer to linguistic reality in the societies across the world which use English".

The prescriptive aspect that discerns standard from non-standard varieties has often been pointed out and defined as discriminatory in that it tends to stigmatize the varieties which are not considered as standard (Milroy/Milroy 2012). Thus, English is here understood as a complex system[6] of varieties consisting of, and deriving from, the interaction of a copious number of factors, such as geographical, social, political, and pragmatic ones.

2.4.2 Defining standard varieties

Defining partially overlapping concepts such as dialect and variety is not unproblematic. A 'variety' commonly refers "to any form of a language which can be sufficiently delimited from another form" (Hickey 2014: 331). However, the identification of a 'sufficient' differentiation is not automatic, given that we often deal with a continuum of language forms.

'Variety' is commonly used to imply a desire to adopt a neutral term, deprived of the connotations which are sometimes associated with 'dialect', a label which tends to be used, in particular, for traditional, older forms of a language (Hickey 2014: 331). McArthur highlights that a dialect is often imprecisely conceived simply as "a geographical subdivision of an established language" (2002: 8). The term dialect is also often assigned a negative connotation and is used to discern a vernacular from a more prestigious or 'exclusive' variety, although the distinction is often opaque. Moreover, in some cases the dialect actually functions as an independent language, as happens with Cantonese (McArthur 2002: 8).

In this work, following a conspicuous body of research, and to avoid any potentially negative associations, the term variety is preferred to the term dialect, as the former covers a wide range of concepts and may be understood as a regional or social form of language, as well as that of a specific community of practice.

Over the centuries, some varieties of English have been labeled as minor, inferior, or impure for various reasons, including the limited number of users, socio-political considerations, or the use of a variety in a developing country. However, these varieties are often codified systems with their own specific rules. Thus, nowadays there is widespread agreement that these varieties should not be considered as solely a by-product of the most widely used varieties, but as forms which, in turn, potentially influence others. Consequently, they represent a factor of enrichment for the English language in that they may contribute to its revitalization.

2.4.3 Pidgins and creoles

Within the debate on the liability of the conceptual borders between standard and non-standard varieties, contact languages[7] also assume a key role. In the case of English-based pidgins and creoles, the question of whether they should be classified as English or not remains open, and their status can be controversial. In broad terms, it is argued that pidgins are contact languages used between speakers of different languages for specific functional purposes, especially for trade, while creoles are spoken as native languages. Initially, a pidgin has a very restricted use, for example for specific commercial purposes; it may, subsequently, evolve into a more extended variety which displays a vaster array of social and pragmatic functions. Transitional stages may occur, sometimes leading to the formation of a creole used as a native language. The process of creolization can be carried out even within a generation and also be accompanied by a period of relative varietal diglossia, where the two forms coexist and are used in different contexts. Finally, a decreolization process may also take place, leading to the abandoning of the creole in favor of a more standard variety.

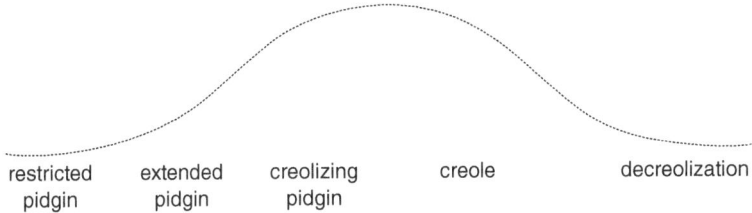

Figure 2.4 Traditional life cycle of a creole

These stages are visually outlined in Figure 2.4, which represents the traditional life cycle of a creole. Clearly, this representation is merely illustrative in that its linearity fails to contemplate the complexity of the dynamics which may develop.

Several theories about the origin of pidgins and creoles have been suggested, and they include the following:

1. The *independent parallel development hypothesis* posits that the similarities between different pidgins and creoles derive from an independent but parallel development, as they all have an Indo-European origin and in some cases share a similar West African substratum.
2. The *nautical jargon hypothesis* theorizes the derivation of pidgin from nautical jargon (see Reinecke 1938).
3. The *monogenetic hypothesis* postulates the existence of a proto-pidgin language, which is often identified as *sabir*, a lingua franca based on Romance languages which developed in the 15th century in the Mediterranean area.

There are also different *universalist hypotheses* which explain similarities between different pidgins and creoles as a universal human tendency to use languages with specific features (e.g. phonological simplicity, SVO syntax, polysemous vocabulary, etc.).

On a final note, it is also worth pointing out that, theoretically and methodologically, World Englishes are generally approached from an ethnolinguistic or sociolinguistic perspective, whereas scholars focusing on pidgins and creoles have the genesis of contact languages as a key point of their research agendas, which often develop within a structural framework. However, the time is ripe for a convergence of the two strains of research, as the study of contact ecologies and New Englishes ecologies can be fruitfully combined in order to observe complex dynamics, such as the effect of substrate influence (see Bao 2018). Thus, WE data can be employed to develop contact-linguistic theories, which in turn can offer new perspectives on the studies of regional varieties.

2.5 The World Englishes ethos

As the English language seems to be spinning faster and faster outwards from its presumed traditional center(s), scholars are confronted by the growing concern that former conceptualizations of English, which have long held sway, need to be reframed. The very notion of language may have to be questioned in that the concept of a discrete entity which can be described in terms of core and variation seems to ignore the dramatically different contexts in which English participates (Makoni/Pennycook 2006).

The divergence from a hypothetical center, if conceptually accepted, is also necessarily accompanied by other multiple forces. Centripetal and centrifugal thrusts coexist and render the constellation of English ever more complex, unstable and in constant evolution.

One of the tenets of this work lies in the awareness that World Englishes now constitute a research paradigm which has been widely explored and amply accepted, but still needs to be continuously problematized given its fluid nature. The vast number of studies published on this topic in the last few decades may generate the feeling that this area of study is to some extent saturated and that new works on the topic may only be reiterations of previous ones. However, investigating World Englishes is important not only in order to gain more accurate descriptions of different varieties, but also to constantly reconceptualize the essence of the English compound and bring new linguistic challenges to the fore.

The paradigm of World Englishes developed as a revolutionary and groundbreaking approach which contested the traditionally established ethos of English as a monolithic entity. Such a traditional philosophy, in turn, represented the expression of a Western-oriented approach and to some extent the heritage of an imperialistic view. Instead, one of the doctrines of the World English ethos is that all varieties are recognized with equal dignity and validity.

The approach to World Englishes often presupposes the existence of varieties which can be investigated in isolation as if they were discrete and distinct entities. More profoundly, instead, the overarching principle should be the acknowledgment that plurality and fluidity lie at the basis of different forms of English. This volume discusses cases focusing on specific geographic regions for the sake of clarity, but also attempts to stress the volatility of borders which exist between languages, and even more so between English varieties, in a process of reciprocal influence and constant cross-contamination and evolution.

If cross-fertilization and dynamism are taken as lenses for looking at the multitude of fluctuating Englishes, a new ethos of World Englishes emerges, in which the objective is not to pinpoint differences but to observe potential and actual reciprocal influences. If a metaphor has to be employed, it would be that of the 'English language ocean', in which different waters and seas may merge, while at the same time being assigned different labels.

Thus, defining a stable paradigm for World Englishes would be a contradiction in terms. Indeed, any investigation of WE should continuously gain momentum in this multifaceted world which is constantly evolving and needs to be unceasingly reconceptualized and expounded. In other words, the acceptance that the concept of World Englishes has now received should not lead to a lack of research impetus. Indeed, new stimuli are much needed if we want to avoid the risk of crystallizing a paradigm which, instead, had in its origins a 'subversive' character, or at least was based on the constant challenge of preconceived models.

Although this work does not specifically develop within the post-varieties research framework (Seargeant/Tagg 2011), it is essential to underline the need to move beyond traditional analyses of World Englishes as discrete units and to embrace a more comprehensive perspective. At the same time, however, the existence of specific sociolinguistic dynamics developing within certain areas or communities of speakers cannot be ignored. Consequently, the two approaches are not mutually exclusive and should be integrated in order to offer a more sophisticated interpretation which takes into account these tensions. I would call this orientation a 'post-WE integrative approach', in that it considers the differences emerging across forms of English but constantly aims to relate them to one another. In other words, this integration does not imply any neglect of the original WE ethos, but rather its reframing within more porous boundaries.

Notes

1 "GlobEng: International Conference on Global English", University of Verona, Italy, 14–16 February 2008.
2 For a detailed and comprehensive description see Onysko 2016.
3 Nevertheless, empirical studies have shown that language behavior in expanding countries, and in those where English is spoken as a foreign language, is not necessarily similar and thus the expanding circle and EFL should not be used synonymously (Edwards/Laporte 2015).
4 Although some of these varieties have been singled out to conduct the cases studies in Chapter 6, one of the tenets of this work is that the boundaries between

one variety of English and another are so blurred, and the contaminations so significant, that labels may appear artificial.
5 Honey's approach may be seen, to some extent, as the precursor of the so-called New Prescriptivism school of thought (see Beal 2009).
6 For a comprehensive discussion of complexity and complex systems see Mitchell 2009.
7 A further discussion of contact languages can be found in Section 6.3, where the Caribbean region is adopted as an exemplificatory case.

Part 2

3 Lexical developments

The dynamic and evolving aspect of languages is now a truism and can be summarized with de Saussure's oft-quoted statement: "Time changes all things; there is no reason why language should escape this universal law" (de Saussure 1959: 78). The lexical characteristics of a language are also subject to constant processes of modification and variation, which are an intrinsic (and inescapable) aspect of the evolution of a natural language. While purists may see variations as a form of contamination and corruption of an established system, it is widely agreed that new word formations, variations, and acquisitions of new meanings are the manifestation of a linguistic need, and of the creative linguistic power of individuals.

In this study, word formation is not only understood as a part of morphology but as a field that somehow transcends exclusively morphological issues (Schmid 2016: 14–15). Indeed, new words, as will be seen, are not necessarily formed through morphological components (as happens in the process of conversion; see Section 4.5). The attention to word formation thus not only includes reflections on derivational morphology but also other lexical productive phenomena.

Before starting to investigate the lexical developments which take place in English varieties, the notion of 'word' adopted in this book should be clarified, given its multifaceted nature. Following a well-established tradition, 'word' is here conceived as an umbrella term (with a certain level of conceptual ambiguity) which covers both word-forms and lexemes[1] (see e.g. Schmid 2016).

'Lexicon' is also a malleable concept and broadly refers to the repertoire used by speakers and which is inevitably a reflection of a specific context and a specific community of practice (Minkova/Stockwell 2006). Thus, it stands to reason that the investigation of lexical developments, and in particular of neologisms, can offer interesting insights into the dynamic aspects of a variety and into a given community of speakers.

36 Lexical developments

The creation of new words often functions as a barometer of the evolution of a language from a socio-cultural perspective. Any language is characterized by constant innovation and continuous changes, and this seems even more evident in the case English, which has reached the status of a global tongue and whose development is also based on reciprocal influences with other tongues.

New terms may derive from the contact between different languages, as well as between specific varieties of a given tongue. The process is ongoing, fluid and at times ephemeral, and defining which words are typical of a certain variety and should be considered as neologisms of the English language, is highly problematic.

From a methodological perspective, a lexical investigation of WE is rendered particularly complex by the permeability of the peripheries between the varieties considered (see Section 2.5). Moreover, as will be seen, the issue related to the acceptance of new words emerging in different varieties remains fundamental. Indeed, as Görlach points out, "the degree to which non-BrE (or other native English) coinages are accepted by the speech community is a gauge of the independence of the variety in question" (Görlach 1995: 79).

Certainly, the role played by World Englishes is crucial for the definition of the English lexicon. Crystal (e.g. 2006) has long noted that the vocabulary of the English language would probably be much larger if we included specific words used in some varieties of English. In line with this consideration, the present study describes some selected varieties focusing on their lexical peculiarities. Hence, this analysis is conducted with the awareness that, even though a term used in a certain variety of English is not included in one of the best-known dictionaries of the English language (e.g. *Oxford English Dictionary*), it does not mean that it is not (or will not be) part of the English vocabulary at large.

3.1 Productivity and creativity

An investigation of the lexicon of a language, and of new word formations, should take into account the concepts of productivity and creativity (see Lyons 1977 for a seminal discussion; see also Aronoff 1983; Bauer 1983, 2001; Lipka 2005; Plag 2006; Hohenhaus 2007; Fernández-Domínguez 2010).

Generally speaking, productivity is defined as rule-governed, while creativity tends to be understood as "any deviation from the productive rules" (Štekauer 2005: 224) and generates "less automatic creations [...] which are clearly deliberate and independent" (Bauer 2005: 329). However, the level of deliberativeness in word usage is often undefinable.

Lexical developments 37

More specifically, the term productivity refers to a feature "which allows a native speaker to produce an infinitely large number of sentences, many (or most) of which have never been produced before", while creativity is understood as "the native speaker's ability to extend the language system in a motivated, but unpredictable (non-rule-governed) way" (Bauer 1983: 63).

However, two main issues seem to emerge. Firstly, as mentioned in Chapter 2, one needs to define and problematize nativeness; secondly, even if we adopt the native versus non-native dichotomy unproblematically, it is not to be excluded that the latter, non-native language users, may be involved in the productive and creative processes. Nevertheless, Bauer's definitions remain fundamental to the understanding of word-formation mechanisms, although the exigencies linked to the use of a global language make these processes extremely multifaceted and fluid. In line with Bauer, Aronoff and Anshen (1998: 242–243) define productivity as "a probabilistic continuum that predicts the use of potential words". Conversely, the notion of unpredictability emphasizes the spontaneous, non-constrained aspect of the creative process (Bauer 2001).

In a similar vein, Plag argues that "the productivity of a word-formation process can be defined as its general potential to be used to create new words and as the degree to which this potential is exploited by the speakers" (Plag 2006: 127). Following Bauer (1983), it can also be stated that productivity develops not only within specific pragmatic and grammatical constraints, but also according to semantic and conceptual restrictions. Broadly speaking, a term should denote an object that is cognitively admissible and perceived as real. This does not mean that abstract concepts are not accepted but that there needs to be a certain degree of cognitive acceptability according to the speaker's concept map. Therefore, different individuals and communities have different acceptability standards and consider a term more or less useful and attractive depending on their mental schemata. Moreover, the acceptance of a new lexeme is based on its perception as necessary on the part of the community (Fernández-Domínguez 2010). For instance, the word *township* in South Africa refers to a black ghetto, and is only used when referring to a specific geographical area. This demonstrates that its acceptance is linked to a given lexical need on the part of the community to designate a specific object/concept.

Studies on productivity have often relied on lexicographic work. However, this exclusive approach appears to neglect the element of potentiality which is inherent in productive processes. In this respect, Booij remarks that, as a dictionary only contains established words, it "is always lagging behind with respect to the use of productive morphological patterns" and, moreover, "morphological productivity manifests itself most clearly in the appearance of complex words that never make it to the dictionary" (Booij 2005: 69).

The use of corpora, although perfectible, shows some advantages, as traditionally illustrated by Baayen and Lieber (1991: 803):

- corpora may contain transparent words which are excluded from dictionaries
- corpora contain only words that appear in naturally occurring speech
- corpora may offer information on the frequency of words.

Given the nature of the notion of productivity, an important advantage of using corpora is that they can offer insightful data into word-formation processes, even (or especially) for words which are not lexicographically recognized yet.

3.2 Investigating neologisms

This study of lexical aspects of English varieties focuses in particular on their innovative aspects. An emphasis on neologisms allows us to gain a finer understanding of recent lexical developments and to show the creative potential of English varieties, as well as the reciprocal influences emerging among them from a lexical perspective.

Intuitively, neologisms are defined as new words or expressions, which may be monolexical and polylexical units. They generally express the need to identify a new concept or idea and may be related to scientific and technological inventions or discoveries, or be a way of labelling specific social and cultural situations.

It is widely agreed that there are diverse reasons behind the birth of a neologism, which may be reduced to external and internal exigencies. More specifically, we can encounter three main cases:

1 A new concept to be defined (as in a new invention)
2 The recontextualization of an existing term
3 Emphatic purposes and an expression of creativity.

The creation of a new word and the acquisition of new meanings for existing words are happening constantly throughout the world, especially given the global reach of the English language. In light of the pervasiveness of English, and its coexistence with other languages within a community or within a country, lexical creativity in English is a critical phenomenon which is crucial to understanding the evolution of the language when seen as an intricate network of interrelated varieties and not as a monolithic unit.

Thus, the lexical approach adopted in this study for the investigation of World Englishes takes into account not only neologisms which are considered typical of a specific region, but also the ones shared by several varieties.

It has often been stated that neologisms are representative of the dynamic aspect of a language or a variety, both synchronically and diachronically (Crystal 1997; Fischer 1998; Hohenhaus 2007). Indeed, any etymological dictionary will be full of revealing examples. The 'novelty' aspect of a neologism is not only based on an absolute temporal criterion. Rather, it depends on several relative factors, such as the specific knowledge of the speakers and their acceptance of the new word, as well as its ability to penetrate different semantic fields and genres (Fischer 1998: 4). Indeed, newness in language has been defined as a predominantly subjective element, as language cannot be stably described within "its limits in the chronological, spatial, and social dimensions" (Rey 1995: 75).

There exist different elements constitutive of a neologism, which is ultimately a multidimensional concept. Following Cabré (1999: 205), four main criteria may be adopted: psychological, lexicographic, diachronic, and semantic (or, more specifically, a criterion linked to formal or semantic instability). Visibly, none of the criteria alone is sufficient in order to define a neologism. For example, the lexicographic aspect is based on the use of dictionaries, which alone cannot be fully satisfactory in that "the apparent objectivity of dictionaries rests on an extensive series of subjective editorial decisions" (Curzan 2000: 96).

Similarly, it may be argued that four main aspects should be considered:

- cognitive recognition
- lexicographic novelty
- social acceptance
- reiterated formation.

In other words, a lexical formation needs to be cognitively recognized as new, should be up to the minute from a lexicographic perspective (e.g. not included in a dictionary), be accepted by a community, and used repeatedly.

This premise calls for a reflection on the nature of neologisms and the processes they undergo. In particular, the insertion of words in a dictionary is a contentious issue. As has been mentioned previously, new terms are being created continuously, for example as an intentional modification (with different pragmatic functions) of existing ones. The inclusion of such terms in a dictionary has to be preceded by a long critical process which primarily aims to evaluate whether or not we are simply dealing with lexical meteors.

Some scholars have developed specific formulas to define the probability for a word to enter the language system in a stable way, and, therefore, the dictionary. For example, Metcalf (2002) suggests the "fudge" formula, where a score from 0 to 2 is assigned to each factor (the higher the total score, the higher the probability of stable inclusion in the language system):

F   frequency
U   unobtrusiveness
D   diversity of users and situations
G   generation of other forms and meanings
E   endurance of the concept to which the word refers.

Similarly, Barnhart (2007) develops the formula $V \times F \times R \times G \times T$, corresponding to:

V   variety of forms
F   frequency
R   references
G   genres
T   time span.

The combination of these factors determines the level of importance of a neologism and is considered when assessing it for dictionary inclusion. However, the use of strictly quantitative factors in order to determine aspects which are qualitative in their very nature (such as the importance of a neologism) is, certainly, perfectible.

Some words may never enter a dictionary but may be used at a specific point in time by a certain community, and these offer precious insights into a specific variety from a sociolinguistic perspective. Therefore, this analysis takes into consideration neologisms which have entered one or more lexicographic resources, as well as terms which have not been selected by lexicographers as new dictionary entries but have still emerged in the corpora investigated.

3.3 From nonce-formations to neologisms

The concept of a neologism is related to that of nonce-formation, which is a word invented by a speaker, very often "on the spur of the moment" (Brinton/Traugott 2005: 45). Thus, a nonce-formation is "actively formed in performance" (Hohenhaus 2007: 18) in order "to meet the immediate needs of a particular communicative situation" (Crystal 2000: 219).

Lexical developments 41

Broadly speaking, if a nonce-formation undergoes a process of institutionalization, it may become a neologism. However, these phenomena develop along a "neological continuum", where the nonce-formation loses its occasional status, is reiterated, and is subsequently recognized more frequently, becoming part of the lexicon understood by (and available to) a greater number of speakers.

In a similar vein, we may talk about the existence of a continuum which includes several stages such as protologism, prelogism, and neologism. More specifically, the term protologism is defined as a "freshly minted word not yet widely accepted" (Epstein 2012: 101); as the name suggests, it is a form of prototype which may disappear if not successful. Alternatively, the word may be adopted by the few, by the many, or by the masses. We may then talk about a prelogism, that is, a word which is (to varying degrees) reiterated and has attained a higher frequency of use. It is in the process of gaining acceptance and may gradually assume the contours of a neologism. Subsequently, a neologism may lose its aspect of novelty and be perceived as a 'stable word'. After a period of time, it may be perceived as an archaism and subsequently as a 'necrologism' (a 'dead' word which has lost acceptance on the part of the speakers). It is also plausible to argue for the existence of 'postlogisms', understood as words that, after having disappeared, make a comeback. This tentative conceptualization of the stages of the life cycle of a word may be schematically outlined as in Figure 3.1 below.

Figure 3.1 has a merely illustrative purpose and displays some obvious limitations. Firstly, no pictorial representation can satisfactorily capture the complexity and the ineffability of lexical change within the efflux of time. Some of the labels chosen are clearly simplifications, used merely for the sake of clarity, and may in turn include a series of other stages. For instance, the word 'archaism' is employed here as an umbrella term covering obsolete, out-of-date, dated, or archaic words (see Peprník 2006: 75). Moreover, there exists the apparent impossibility of offering a neat distinction between the various

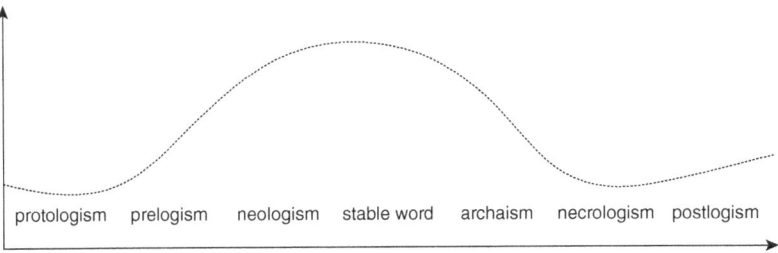

Figure 3.1 Potential stages of the life cycle of a word

phases as, for instance, some may not take place, while others may overlap. Words may enter the language, be relinquished, and then make a comeback, assuming the same meaning or being characterized by a semantic shift. In addition, languages display words which have remained unswerving over extended periods of time.

The process of establishment of a neologism, following Bauer (1983, 2001), includes lexicalization and institutionalization. The former generally relates to structural affirmation, whereas the latter tends to represent a form of socio-cultural and pragmatic affirmation (Bauer 1983, 2001).

According to Schmid (2008: 1–36), the establishment phase, describable as a diachronic development of a word, may be observed from three different perspectives (see also Kerremans 2015):

1   Lexicalization (from a structural perspective) is the structural development of the term. It refers to "the creation of a nonce-form which serves to express a new meaning" (Schmid 2008: 4). The word or the expression gradually assumes semantic autonomy, observable from a diachronic perspective.
2   Institutionalization (from a socio-pragmatic perspective) is defined by Lipka et al. (2004: 8) as "the integration of a lexical item, with a particular form and meaning, into the existing stock of words as a generally accepted and current lexeme". This concept brings with it a semantic acceptance which goes beyond strict context dependence.
3   Hypostatization (from a cognitive perspective) is based on the cognitive consolidation of the neologism in the mind of the speakers. It is the process through which a lexical unit becomes part of the mental lexicon (Schmid 2008).

These phases are not always distinctly separable as concepts, and do not clearly develop at differing times from a diachronic perspective. The process does not necessarily have a clear beginning and end, but may circularly repeat itself. It may also not regard all the speakers of a particular community in the same timeframe, involving a restricted number of speakers initially. Therefore, the process of establishment within the community is not seen as concluded, but may subsequently extend to other speakers and become more widespread, allowing the term to be defined as an established neologism only over time.

This process is even more labyrinthine when dealing with a language with the global reach of English. Indeed, can the establishment of a word within a small variety of speakers be seen as equal to its establishment in the English language as such? In this respect, lexicalization and institutionalization are not automatically linked to cognitive recognition and acceptance by different communities of speakers. Consequently, some speakers may recognize a word and see it as deviant from their standards of English and reject its use.

On a terminological note, whether these issues arising between different varieties of English should be considered intra-linguistic or inter-linguistic (depending on the importance attributed to factors such as intelligibility) remains an open question. More neutrally, they may be defined as inter-varietal issues.

Starting from the idea of *topicality,* according to which a lexical formation may be used in relation to current affairs for a brief period (Fischer 1998: 16), we can infer that some lexemes arise to express a precise meaning at a specific point in time, but may not become institutionalized. Therefore, it is arguable that, potentially, the level of topicality may differ across the varieties of a language. Hence, a word may be used in a certain context for a brief period of time and then be abandoned. However, it may survive in another variety and undergo the process of institutionalization. This happens, for instance, when speakers of a variety lose interest in a term which does not refer to a concept which is perceived as current or valuable for extra-linguistic reasons (see Section 3.1). If, within a variety, other preferred synonymic, quasi-synonymic, or alternative expressions are preferred (e.g. because of higher levels of perceived easiness or appropriateness), the lexicalization process may not be followed by the institutionalization one. This interpretation based on the dissimilar evolution of lexical formations in World Englishes is clearly founded on the assumption that every variety is an autonomous system with its own rules and regularities, and cannot be interpreted simply as inferior in comparison to a presumed supra-variety.

From a theoretical perspective, the social acceptance of a neologism goes through a process of conventionalization. It is commonly agreed that a convention is a standard shared, regularly and systematically, by a community (Clark 1996: 70–71; see also Croft 2000). Conventionalization is based on a series of processes such as innovation, diffusion or propagation, and normation (Milroy 1992: 169; Croft 2000). These processes may vary according to specific social groups and develop in diverse ways in communities speaking different varieties of English. For instance, the process of normation may be implicit, through a tacit socio-cultural agreement, or be more explicitly prescribed through, for instance, prescriptive texts (see Holmes 2008).

The normation process of a lexical unit, understood as an implicit or explicit form of standardization, may be resisted by those who feel that it is not representative of their identity. The new word may be intentionally rejected in order to leave space for others which are perceived as more identitarian. Similarly, a widely accepted lexeme within a variety may be considered erroneous in other varieties where it is ignored, or even appears dangerous by potentially blighting the purity of the language.

From a cognitive point of view, considerable scholarly attention has been devoted to the investigation of how speakers analyze, memorize, and use neological formations (see Gaskell/Dumay 2003; de Vaan et al. 2007; Davis et al. 2009). Gaskell and Dumay (2003: 106) focus on how neologisms "are integrated into the listener's mental lexicon". They define this specific process as lexicalization.[2] They demonstrate that speakers are able to recognize a new word formation after a few contacts, but they need several contacts before that can influence their mental lexicon.

Through their empirical research, de Vaan et al. (2007) conclude that speakers can identify a neologism quite quickly, at its second occurrence, even if its meaning is not always understood perfectly. Also, context plays a fundamental role in interpreting and memorizing a neologism as it helps the identification of the word in future, similar situations.

According to Schmid (2008), a pseudo-concept turns into a gestalt when it is recognized as a unit with conceptual substance. Although exposure does not guarantee permanent entrenchment, with higher exposure the word is etched more deeply into the speaker's mental lexicon and is more liable to become entrenched. Thus, the social and cognitive planes appear strictly interrelated. In this respect, the entrenchment-and-conventionalization framework developed by Schmid (2014) is particularly illuminating in that it describes lexical innovation as rooted in, and triggered by, social and cognitive factors involving individual speakers, as well as discourse communities and society at large.

Notes

1 For the sake of clarity, a lexeme may be defined as "a unit of lexical meaning, which exists regardless of any inflectional endings it may have or the number of words it may contain. [. . .] The headwords in a dictionary are all lexemes" (Crystal 2003: 118). For instance, *work* and *works* are seen as word-forms of the lexeme *work*.
2 In their view, this term assumes a cognitive perspective rather than a structural one (as suggested by Schmid 2008).

4 Word-formation processes

The English lexicon may be understood as "mixed" from a compositional point of view, rather than strictly Germanic (see Crystal 2011), because the language systems that constitute a lexical resource for the English language are several. Certainly, this is true for other languages too, but it is visibly manifest in English and its varieties. Indeed, its global aspect, and the numerous substrata and noticeable influences which characterize different countries and communities of speakers all over the world, render the hybridity of the English lexicon evident. For instance, borrowings and loanwords from other tongues may become part of the English lexical repertoire. Inter-varietal borrowing and loanwords also represent an interesting phenomenon, in that words which develop within a certain variety may subsequently spread to other varieties. A word is often adopted in the same form, but may potentially be modified, following the same dynamics that inter-linguistic borrowing undergoes.

While some of the processes (e.g. borrowing, semantic drift, conversion, or eponymy) do not technically imply the formation of new lexemes from morphological elements, others however do (e.g. composites). Thus, word formation is not necessarily morphematic or related to derivational morphology. In particular, non-morphematic word formation can be described as "any word-formation process that is not morpheme-based [. . .], that is, which uses at least one element which is not a morpheme; this element can be a splinter, a phonæstheme, part of a syllable, an initial letter, a number or a letter used as a symbol" (Fandrych 2004: 18).

When dealing with neologisms, we may also encounter new items intended as creations *ex nihilo*. These formations are novel and non-deducible (Bauer 1983: 239) and are comparatively rare. Neologisms are generally based on more economical processes from a linguistic and cognitive perspective.

With the aim of attempting to offer a definition of neologisms, one can draw on Newmark's seminal work in which neologisms are described as "*newly* coined *lexical units* or *existing lexical units that acquire* a *new sense*" (Newmark 1988: 140). In his classic study focusing on the translation of neologisms, Newmark proposed twelve types of neologisms:

A   Existing lexical items with new senses:

   1   Words
   2   Collocations.

B   New forms:

   1   New coinages
   2   Derived words
   3   Abbreviations
   4   Collocations
   5   Eponyms
   6   Phrasal words
   7   Transferred words (new and old referents)
   8   Acronyms (new and old referents)
   9   Pseudo-neologisms
   10 Internationalisms.

The lexical categories analyzed in this work partially draw on Newmark (1988) but mainly follow the classic categorization of word-formation processes as offered by Algeo (1980). More specifically, the main categories suggested by Algeo are: composites, shifts, shortenings, loanwords, and blends.

Similarly, the main processes taken into account in this analysis are the following:

1   Composites:

   a   Affixation
   b   Compounding

2   Abbreviations:

   a   Acronyms and initialisms
   b   Clipping

3   Blends
4   Borrowing
5   Conversion
6   Semantic drift
7   Eponyms.

These processes will now be described in more detail.[1]

4.1 Composites

4.1.1 Affixation

Affixation is a common type of word-formation process which, in its simplest terms, consists of adding an affix (e.g. prefix, suffix, infix, or circumfix) to a root. However, as Plag stresses, "it is not always obvious whether something should be regarded as a root or an affix" (Plag 2003: 90). Indeed, as he notes, affixes such as *-free, -less, -like, and -wise* may be used as suffixes, as well as being free morphemes which occur on their own.

It should also be noted that a distinction can be made between bases, stems and roots. According to Bauer (2001), 'base' is a more general term which includes both roots and stems. A stem is the word-form which remains after the deletion of inflectional affixes (e.g. in the form *chairs*, the stem is *chair*), while a root is the word-form which remains after the deletion of any affix, inflectional or derivational (e.g. in the form *undefinable*, the root is *define*).

Following Bauer (2001), affixes can be involved in two different processes: inflection and derivation. Inflection does not imply a change in meaning or word class, and generally inflectional affixes affect elements such as tense, person, number, or case. For instance, the *-ed* affix used in past forms is inflectional. Instead, derivation creates new lexemes which often belong to a new word class. Among the numerous examples available, we can mention the suffix *-ful*. However, in some cases, for example with negative prefixes such as *un-*, the word class remains the same. As there is theoretically no specific limit to the number of derivational affixes, it is clear that they play a key role in terms of lexical creativity and innovation.

Infixes are used quite rarely in the creation of terms, whereas prefixes and suffixes are more productive. Prefixation implies the use of a bound lexical morpheme as the first constituent and a free lexical morpheme as a second constituent (e.g. *dislike*). Prefixes do not usually modify the grammatical category of a word, and among the most common prefixes we have *de-* and *re-*. Interestingly, new terms related to modern technologies sometimes present interchangeable possibilities. For instance, the action of deleting a contact from a list of friends on a social network may be *to unfriend* or *to defriend*. As Connor Martin (2014) notes, *to unfriend* is used more than four times as frequently and appeared earlier chronologically. However, they are both commonly used.

Suffixes (be they nominal, verbal, adjectival, or adverbial; see Plag 2003: 86–98) do not only change the form of a word but may also change its grammatical category. Some of the most productive suffixes in English are: *-dom*, *-ess*, *-ation*, *-ness*, *-ize*, *-less*, *-able* and *-ly*. Another common one is the agentive suffix *-er*, which develops into a vast range of meanings beyond the typically agentive one, such as instrumental, causal, locative, and patient.

4.1.2 Compounding

New words can be formed through compounding, which ultimately refers to the "merging of two or more words" (Manning/Schütze 1999: 83). In this respect, Plag emphasizes the binary nature of a compound, as even multi-unit elements can be divided into binary units (Plag 2003: 173).

According to Schmid, prototypical compounds are characterized by a specific semantic structure in which the head is modified, or specified by a modifier (2016: 121). Consequently, the head may be seen as a hypernym of the compound itself. Thus, *showroom* is considered a hyponym of the superordinate *room*. These forms are also called endocentric compounds (Schmid 2016: 123; see Bauer 1983: 203). Conversely, in exocentric compounds the head is not the semantic core of the word which is modified by the modifier (e.g. *greenback*, *paperback*) (see Schmid 2016: 125).

Within compounds, Plag identifies neoclassical compounds, which are "those forms in which lexemes of Latin or Greek origin are combined to form new combinations that are not attested in the original languages" (Plag 2003: 198). Neoclassical elements in initial positions are, for instance: *auto-*, *pseudo-*, *retro-*, *theo-*, or modern ones such as *ultra-*, *hyper-*, and *cyber-*. Elements generally used in final position are: *-cide*, *-logy*, and *-phile*. Neoclassical forms are not free morphemes and need to be linked to other words. Furthermore, they cannot be defined as affixes, can be linked together, and do not necessarily need a root (e.g. *telescope*).

Other types of compounds[2] are:

- copulative compounds (e.g. *bitter-sweet*) where the parts display a similar level of importance for the formation of the word
- genitive compounds (e.g. *teacher's book*)
- particle compounds (e.g. *into*) which are constituted by grammatical, rather than lexical, morphemes. Given the lack of lexical function it may be argued that they are not ascribable to the world of compounds, but they still represent a complex lexeme from a morphological perspective (Schmid 2016: 128).

4.2 Abbreviations

For the purpose of this study, following Algeo (1980), abbreviations are used as a superordinate term, which includes acronyms and initialisms as well as clippings.

4.2.1 Acronyms and initialisms

Plag (2003) defines acronyms and initialisms as forms of abbreviations and specifies that acronyms are pronounced as a single word whereas initialisms (also called alphabetisms) are pronounced as a series of letters. Acronyms and initialisms may be in widespread usage (e.g. *www*, *IT*, *HTML*) or be used only in a particular variety of English (see *TIBS*, Trans-Island Bus Service, or *PAP*, People's Action Party, used in Singaporean English). It should be noted that backronyms (or bacronyms) also exist. They are reverse acronyms, that is, phrases constructed with the aim of creating an acronym which may fit an existing word. For instance, the *Apple Lisa* desktop computer was originally named after Steve Jobs' daughter, although later the phrase Local Integrated Software Architecture was coined.

4.2.2 Clipping

Clipping refers to the shortening of a word, which does not generally cause a variation from a semantic and grammatical perspective. Backclipping (or apocope) refers to the deletion of the final part of a word, whereas foreclipping (or apharesis) concerns the omission of the initial part. Terms such as *flu* (from *influenza*) are sometimes referred to as fore-and-aft clipping. Clipped abbreviations may be counted as neologisms, although some are so widespread as to have lost their aura of novelty. While some are commonly used in different varieties (*prof* for *professor*, *fax* for *facsimile*), others are typical of certain varieties, such as *beaut* for *beautiful* in Australian English (AUE). Clipped abbreviations may also be accompanied by further specific variations, for example *arvo* in AUE for *afternoon*. Aphetic forms may also be seen as a particular type of abbreviation in which the initial unstressed syllable is omitted (e.g. *'cause* for *because*).

4.3 Blends

The process of lexical blending has been subject to different definitions. In its basic interpretation, the minimal requirement is the merger of two source lexemes, of which at least one is clipped. Oft-quoted examples are *smog* or *motel*. Algeo (1977) defines blends (or portmanteau words) as "compounds which are composed of one word and part of another, or part of two (and occasionally three) other words" (1977: 48). In this study, I adopt a broader definition of blends as words which usually consist of a word and a splinter or two splinters (Lehrer 2007: 115–116), even though the lexemes involved may be more than two.

This process has been particularly in use since the 1930s (Ayto 2004) and the creation of new blends continues to increase. A wide range of blends have emerged across different varieties of English. One oft-quoted example is the blend *Singlish* (Singaporean English). Similarly, the word *Spanglish*[3] commonly depicts the blending process between Spanish and English.

Bauer (2006) states that clipping must involve two source lexemes in a blend; Plag (2003) also emphasizes the importance of a semantic criterion, according to which the clipped lexemes are in a coordinate relation (excluding therefore relations such as modifier–head).

4.4 Borrowing

From a formal perspective, a classical distinction is usually made between a loanword and a calque. Smead (1998) describes the former as a transfer of meaning and form, while the latter is fundamentally a transfer of meaning (Smead 1998; see also Haugen 1950: 212–220). A calque is thus defined as a loan-translation.[4]

Over the years English has borrowed words from several languages.[5] Some loanwords have now entered all varieties of English, such as *kindergarten* (from German) and *sushi* (from Japanese). *Aloha* (from Hawaiian) can also be found in most varieties but is more common in Hawaiian English. Similarly, some Spanish loanwords which were originally borrowed from the Aztec language, such as *avocado* or *tequila*, are now familiar to most English speakers. Others may be known mainly to speakers living in a particular geographical area (e.g. *cholla*, which may be in more common usage among people living in the south-eastern states of the USA; see Akmajian et al. 2010: 30).

Neological formation often derives from contact between different languages. For example, from a lexical perspective the evolution of American English[6] was inevitably influenced by the indigenous languages.[7] Local languages provided several loanwords, often related to fauna (e.g. *opossum*), flora (e.g. *squash*), or cultural and everyday terms such as *moccasin* or *totem*. After the American Revolution, expansion west led to the introduction of new coinages, based on loanwords, especially deriving from contacts with native Spanish speakers. Examples are *rodeo*, *guerrilla* (Spanish for 'small war'), *alligator* (from *el lagarto*, 'the lizard'), and *cafeteria* (from *cafetería*, 'coffee store').

From a sociolinguistic perspective, it should be remembered that the term 'borrowing' is rather complex, and a distinction can be made between borrowing and imposition, where the latter identifies a process in which the features of a first language are transferred into a second language. The lexical choice is therefore imposed due to practical constraints (Winford 2010: 170).

Another classic distinction also exists between borrowing which involves national languages versus "dialect borrowing" (Bloomfield 1933: 444–445). Despite the need to problematize the concept of dialect from a contemporary perspective (see Chapter 2), inter-varietal borrowing (as opposed to inter-linguistic borrowing) is also relevant to the nature of this work.

4.5 Conversion

Conversion is "an extremely productive process" (Plag 1999: 219) which, despite maintaining the unaltered form of a word, creates a new lexical item (Balteiro 2007: 13). More specifically, conversion is seen by Plag (2003) as an instance of derivation without affixation. It is "the use of a form which is regarded as being basically of one form class as though it were a member of a different word class, without any concomitant change in form" (Bauer 1983: 227). It can be a functional shift in that, generally, it does not affect the meaning of a word. Famous examples are IT words such as *to google*, derived from the noun *Google*, *to tweet*, etc.

Although conversion predominantly involves a change from one word class to another, it can also be with regard to a variation within the same class. This is the case with uncountable–countable nouns (e.g. *coffee–coffees*) or transitive–intransitive verbs (e.g. *fly*).

4.6 Semantic drift

Over time, words may acquire a new meaning and therefore create neologisms from a semantic perspective. Semantic drift or shift is thus "a change in the meaning of a word, with a possible change in syntactic category" (Cook 2010: 16). This (generally diachronic) phenomenon may take place in distinct phases and the new meaning acquired by a word may coexist with the previous one for a certain amount of time (Wilkins 1996). A typical example is *epic*, which was originally related to the epic literary genre but has subsequently been used to also mean 'impressive'.

Among the different types of semantic shifts, we can find ameliorations and pejorations, defined as "common linguistic processes through which the meaning of a word changes to have a more positive or negative evaluation, respectively, in the mind of the speaker" (Cook 2010: 92). Other types of semantic drifts are widening/narrowing, as well as figures of speech such as metaphor, metonymy, synecdoche, hyperbole, and litotes. More precisely, the attribution of a new meaning to an existing signifier has also been defined as semantic neology, whereas the notion of formal neology generally refers to the formation of a new lexifier.[8]

4.7 Eponyms

Eponyms are generally categorized as a specific word-formation process, but could also be understood as a form of semantic drift. In this case, the variation between different varieties of a language may be particularly significant. For instance, the word *durex,* while sometimes used to refer to a condom in British and other varieties of English, can be a generic term for adhesive tape in AUE, even though this meaning is now decreasing.

The concept of eponyms is here used interchangeably with that of "generified words" (Akmajian et al. 2010: 28). Indeed, Akmajian et al. (2010) use examples such as *Kleenex* and *Xerox* to illustrate the 'generification' process through which a proper noun, or a specific brand name, can assume a more common meaning.

Notes

1 Their brief illustration is functional to the full appreciation of some of the word-formation processes described in Chapter 6.
2 For a further discussion of types of compounds see Schmid (2016: 121–131).
3 The term *Spanglish* may be interpreted differently and can be assigned a positive connotation related to bicultural identity (Zentella 2008: 6) or be used pejoratively to indicate an inaccurate mixture of English and Spanish. This word has long been part of linguistic discussion (Stavans 2000; Fairclough 2003; Rothman/Rell 2005).
4 As an oft-quoted example, *loanword* is itself a calque of the German word *Lehnwort*.
5 Loanwords are taken from a donor language and enter the recipient language through contact. English itself is not only a recipient language but also a donor language for most tongues in the world.
6 It is now a truism that American English cannot be seen as a monolithic entity in that it encompasses different varieties, but the term will occasionally be used in this work for the sake of conciseness.
7 It is estimated that in the 16th century there were more than sixty indigenous language families in the USA, but their number has been gradually halved, and most of the remaining languages are today considered endangered.
8 In the case of loanwords, we talk about a formal process in that the new formation is a new signifier in a given language system.

5 Methodological approach

5.1 Approaches to the study of neologisms

A wide range of approaches have been adopted in order to investigate neologisms. While, in the past, the search for and analysis of neologisms were mainly manual, now the preliminary approach is predominantly automatic or semiautomatic. For instance, Veale and Butnariu (2010) investigate neologisms using the automatic search tool Zeitgeist. This enables them to examine neologisms which are present online, comparing formations which appear on Wikipedia to the corresponding ones on the electronic dictionary, WordNet (Miller 1995). In their study, the scholars conclude that just over half the neologisms found on Wikipedia have a connection with a term available on WordNet, and affirm that Wikipedia is a valuable resource for the study of contemporary neologisms.

Levchenko (2010) analyses neological formations and investigates their usage in various media using the assumption that the neologisms have already reached a certain status in order to be used in the press and are, therefore, in the final phase of the establishment process. O'Donovan and O'Neil (2008) suggest the use of tools which compare a reference corpus, consisting of magazines, newspapers, and websites appearing in a specific time period, with a test corpus of texts taken from the same sources but produced during a previous interval. The system proves useful in identifying new formations but becomes problematic when identifying new acquisitions of meaning on the part of existing terms (Cook 2010: 39). Other empirical strategies refer to the search for key words such as *called*, *labelled*, or *defined*, which may be accompanied by neological formations. The investigation of productivity may also take into account speakers' intuition from a psychological perspective, for instance through the use of elicitation tests (see Plag 1999; Schröder/Mühleisen 2010).

The aim of this book is to investigate neologisms across different varieties, trying to combine corpus perspectives with what is ultimately a qualitative approach. Thus, words are observed in terms of formation processes, and special attention is paid to morphological patterns. This is then integrated with reflections on the social and pragmatic implications of such formations.

The discussion focuses not only on those terms which are typical of a specific variety and which display peculiarities from a cultural perspective, but also on their cross-fertilization potential and on how they circulate across varieties.

5.2 Corpora

Following the growing interest in corpus linguistics, several corpora of English have been compiled in the last few decades. While some focus predominantly on the so-called native varieties, others have devoted considerable attention to different world varieties. Clearly, corpora are not exempt from potential limitations. Firstly, one has to deal with the ontological dilemma related to the clear separation of WE into discrete entities. Moreover, from an empirical standpoint, in the case of corpora of WE, the encoding standards may be absent and there may be no agreed spelling system (McEnery/Ostler 2000). However, corpus materials may still be employed as fruitful sources of data, although the unstable nature of some varieties calls for a higher accuracy in the analytic and hermeneutic process.

For practical reasons, this investigation is limited to selected varieties included in ICE (International Corpus of English)[1] and in GloWbE (Corpus of Global Web-based English),[2] so that the analysis can be based on established available corpora. In particular, for the purpose of this work, the varieties which have been taken into account are:

- Nigeria
- East Africa (Kenya and Tanzania)
- South Africa[3]
- Singapore
- Hong Kong
- The Philippines
- India
- Jamaica.

Beyond the above-mentioned corpora, in some specific cases other material (taken, for example, from newspaper articles and the Internet) has also been consulted in order to investigate the use of certain neologisms or to corroborate, or test, observations about a specific word. Therefore, the press and the Internet are also used as a source of data.[4]

A substantial amount of literature has dealt with the possibility of using the web as a corpus in linguistic research (e.g. Hundt et al. 2007). For the purpose of this study, the web is not primarily employed as a corpus intended to provide reliable statistical data or information, but search engines are occasionally employed to investigate the usage of specific neologisms and to gain insights into their semantic value and socio-cultural implications.

The ICE project started in 1988 (Greenbaum 1996) and the corpus consists of several subcorpora of English varieties, such as Canada, East Africa, Great Britain, Hong Kong, India, Ireland and SPICE Ireland,[5] Jamaica, New Zealand, Nigeria (written), the Philippines, Singapore, Sri Lanka (written), USA (written).

All subcorpora amount to approximately one million words and are highly comparable in that they all follow the same structure which includes 500 texts consisting of around 2,000 words each. The majority of texts present are in written form, but spoken ones are also included. The corpora in ICE have been annotated at three levels, namely:

- textual markup
- word-class tagging
- syntactic parsing.

We can see that, not only within 'standard English' but also within many varieties, a diverse spectrum of usage is present (Svartvik/Leech 2016), varying from speech to writing, with different degrees of spontaneity, interactivity and informativeness. This corpus is not limited to a specific mode of usage, and its outline[6] is presented in Table 5.1.[7]

A more recent corpus developed for the study of World Englishes is GloWbE, which consists of 1.9 billion words present in 1.8 million web pages. The corpus includes twenty subcorpora whose composition is illustrated in Table 5.2.[8]

In this study, GloWbE proves useful for verifying and corroborating purposes. It can also be profitably used for comparisons as it efficiently provides comparative data. For instance, from a lexical perspective, one can search for any word or phrase and verify its frequency in all the subcorpora. Comparisons can also be conducted automatically across groups of countries, for example in South Asia. This feature is particularly convenient when investigating the reciprocal lexical influences which may emerge across varieties spoken within a certain macroregion, and to test the hypothesis of the very existence of macrovarieties (see Section 6.4). Given its size, GloWbE is a precious tool for the analysis of regional lexical features. Moreover, it covers a range of 22 varieties, some of which are not included in any other scholarly corpus available for public perusal.

Methodological approach

Table 5.1 ICE corpus design

SPOKEN (300)	Dialogues (180)	Private (100)	Face-to-face conversations (90)
			Phonecalls (10)
		Public (80)	Classroom lessons (20)
			Broadcast discussions (20)
			Broadcast interviews (10)
			Parliamentary debates (10)
			Legal cross-examinations (10)
			Business transactions (10)
	Monologues (120)	Unscripted (70)	Spontaneous commentaries (20)
			Unscripted speeches (30)
			Demonstrations (10)
			Legal presentations (10)
		Scripted (50)	Broadcast news (20)
			Broadcast talks (20)
			Non-broadcast talks (10)
WRITTEN (200)	Non-printed (50)	Student writing (20)	Student essays (10)
			Exam scripts (10)
		Letters (30)	Social letters (15)
			Business letters (15)
	Printed (150)	Academic writing (40)	Humanities (10)
			Social sciences (10)
			Natural sciences (10)
			Technology (10)
		Popular writing (40)	Humanities (10)
			Social sciences (10)
			Natural sciences (10)
			Technology (10)
		Reportage (20)	Press news reports (20)
		Instructional writing (20)	Administrative writing (10)
			Skills/hobbies (10)
		Persuasive writing (10)	Press editorials (10)
		Creative writing (20)	Novels and short stories (20)

The unquestioned scientific validity of ICE is confirmed by the increasing number of research projects based on its usage. However, a project focusing on lexical innovation may require larger databases. With this in mind, the Global Web-based English Corpus can instead be considered as a big-data-based corpus.

Both ICE and GloWbE have strengths and weaknesses alone. However, when working in tandem, their combination of data has been deemed appropriate for the purpose of this study. In particular, GloWbE has a corpus size which is 150 times greater than that of ICE. On the other

Table 5.2 GloWbE outline

Code	General (may also include blogs)			Blogs (only)			Total		
	Web sites	Web pages	Words	Web sites	Web pages	Words	Web sites	Web pages	Words
US	43,249	168,771	253,536,242	48,116	106,385	133,061,093	82,260	275,156	386,809,355
CA	22,178	81,644	90,846,732	16,745	54,048	43,814,827	33,776	135,692	134,765,381
GB	39,254	232,428	255,672,390	35,229	149,413	131,671,002	64,351	381,841	387,615,074
IE	12,978	75,432	80,530,794	5,512	26,715	20,410,027	15,840	102,147	101,029,231
AU	19,619	81,683	104,716,366	13,516	47,561	43,390,501	28,881	129,244	148,208,169
NZ	11,202	54,862	58,698,828	4,970	27,817	22,625,584	14,053	82,679	81,390,476
IN	11,217	76,609	68,032,551	9,289	37,156	28,310,511	18,618	113,765	96,430,888
LK	3,307	25,310	33,793,772	1,672	13,079	12,760,726	4,208	38,389	46,583,115
PK	3,070	25,852	38,005,985	2,899	16,917	13,332,245	4,955	42,769	51,367,152
BD	4,415	30,813	28,700,158	2,332	14,246	10,922,869	5,712	45,059	39,658,255
SG	5,775	28,332	29,229,186	4,255	17,127	13,711,412	8,339	45,459	42,974,705
MY	6,225	29,302	29,026,896	4,591	16,299	13,357,745	8,966	45,601	42,420,168
PH	6,169	28,391	29,758,446	5,979	17,951	13,457,087	10,224	46,342	43,250,093
HK	6,720	27,896	27,906,879	2,892	16,040	12,508,796	8,740	43,936	40,450,291
SA	7,318	28,271	31,683,286	4,566	16,993	13,645,623	10,308	45,264	45,364,498
NG	3,448	23,329	30,622,738	2,072	13,956	11,996,583	4,516	37,285	42,646,098
GH	3,161	32,189	27,644,721	1,053	15,162	11,088,160	3,616	47,351	38,768,231
KE	4,222	31,166	28,552,920	2,073	14,796	12,480,777	5,193	45,962	41,069,085
TZ	3,829	27,533	24,883,840	1,414	13,823	10,253,840	4,575	41,356	35,169,042
JM	3,049	30,928	28,505,416	1,049	15,820	11,124,273	3,488	46,748	39,663,666
Tot	220,405	1,140,741	1,300,348,146	170,224	651,304	583,923,681	340,619	1792,045	1,885,632,973

58 *Methodological approach*

hand, the ICE corpus contains approximately one million words for each of the varieties, which are thus intuitively comparable. However, GloWbE allows automatic normalization of data, therefore guaranteeing fast and accurate comparability.

Although the size of the ICE corpus is adequate for linguistic analysis, a study on lexical innovation benefits from a larger corpus given the expected low frequency of neologisms. Indeed, for high frequency syntactic constructions, ICE is an appreciated and consolidated source of data, but for the investigation of phenomena gravitating around the sphere of lexical innovation bigger corpora are more appropriate. On the other hand, the ICE subcorpora include spoken texts, whereas GloWbE is based on material from the Internet. Although approximately 60 percent of such material is drawn from blogs which make use of informal language, investigating spoken discourse is clearly crucial for the analysis of new lexical items, and the types of genres represented in ICE are more heterogeneous.

No contrastive statistical considerations are offered in relation to the two corpora for various reasons. Firstly, a temporal gap exists between the texts in ICE (whose collection started mainly in the 1990s) and those in GloWbE (2012–2013). Secondly, the genres included are different, and thus potentially lead to incomparable results. Indeed, ICE includes up to 32 different text types, while GloWbE is based predominantly on blogs, newspapers, magazines, and websites. Although the creation of GloWbE approximately followed the approach adopted in ICE (Davies/Fuchs 2015: 4), data also show that the two corpora have a considerably differing ratio of conversational and formal text types (Loureiro-Porto 2017). Although blogs display a high level of informality, they cannot be used as a source of data which is interchangeable with spoken conversation (see Mair 2015: 30–31; Peters 2015: 42).

Thus, ICE and GloWbE represent precious sources of data, but one has to be conscious of their differences, especially when conducting statistical comparisons. For instance, Loureiro-Porto (2017) offers an interesting evaluation of the presence and relative frequency of regional features in selected varieties.[9] The scholar lists, among others, the following regional lexical features typical of Indian, Singapore, and Hong Kong Englishes:[10]

- INE: *brahminhood, burning-ghat, cooliedom, cow eater, crore, elder to, eve tease, goondaism, keep in view, kotwali, lakh, out of station, sacred ash, upliftment*
- SGE: *catch no ball, chin chai, irregardless, sayang, shophouse*
- HKE: *black hand, bno, body check, chim sticks, domestic helper, dragon boat, kwailo, lai see, lucky money, sandwich class, tai tai, triad, typhoon shelter, yum cha.*

Methodological approach 59

The presence of typically Indian English (INE) words in the two corpora is outlined in Table 5.3. Similarly, Table 5.4 shows the frequency of Singapore English (SGE) words. Finally, the frequency of Hong Kong English (HKE) lexical items is illustrated in Table 5.5.

These tables compare the presence of selected lexical items in the respective sections of GloWbE and ICE. Comparisons are made possible due to the use of the log-likelihood value (Rayson 2008). More specifically, a positive value implies overuse in GloWbE, while a negative value implies an underuse in GloWbE. The data show that most items are overused in ICE, except for *lakh* (INE), *yum cha, dragon boat,* and *domestic helper* (HKE). It is plausible to assume that the nature of the text types included in the two corpora may influence statistical comparison, and Loureiro-Porto (2017)

Table 5.3 Raw frequencies of lexical items and log-likelihood value (INE)

	GLoWbE-INE	ICE-INE	Log-likelihood value
brahminhood	1	0	–
burning-ghat	19	0	–
cooliedom	1	0	–
cow eater	1	0	–
crore	11,613	151	−7.1
elder to	26	1	−1.14
eve teas*	71	2	−1.45
goondaism	16	0	–
keep in view	14	5	−24.18
kotwali	22	0	–
lakh	6,791	66	0.28
out of station	23	5	−19.99
sacred ash	14	0	–
upliftment	172	5	−3.82

Table 5.4 Raw frequencies of lexical items and log-likelihood value (SGE)

	GLoWbE-SGE	ICE-SGE	Log-likelihood value
catch no ball	2	0	–
chin chai	2	0	–
irregardless	36	1	−0.03
sayang	55	2	−0.34
shophouse	69	9	−15.49

60 Methodological approach

Table 5.5 Raw frequencies of lexical items and log-likelihood value (HKE)

	GLoWbE-HKE	ICE-HKE	Log-likelihood value
black hand	4	1	−2.64
bno	19	8	−27.7
body check	9	0	–
chim sticks	2	0	–
domestic helper	289	2	5.11
dragon boat	272	3	2.56
kwailo	1	0	–
lai see	35	2	−1.05
lucky money	12	0	–
sandwich class	6	12	−66.77
tai tai	26	0	–
triad	198	13	−8.87
typhoon shelter	47	5	−6.62
yum cha	48	1	0.03

suggests that Internet material generally has a more global nature than other text types, thus reducing the frequency of regional vocabulary in comparison with spoken conversation.

For these reasons, the analysis of the lexical items offered in this study is not based on statistical comparisons between the two corpora, which are instead used predominantly as sources of examples in context.

5.3 Lexicographic resources

Lexicographic reflections are also essential to understanding the evolution of a neologism from an intra-varietal or an inter-varietal perspective. For a new word to be included in a dictionary, certain criteria must be considered, such as the frequency of usage, the number of users, and the usefulness of the word (see Crystal 2006; Barnhart 2007). Certainly, some words may never reach a level of conventionalization, for instance because they are used only by a niche of speakers (see Lehrer 2003; Young 2006).

In the analytical chapter, lexicographic resources, and in particular the *Oxford English Dictionary* (OED), are used to observe how lemmas which are assigned a specific label in terms of provenience (from WE) enter dictionaries and become part of the linguistic repertoire at large.

In this respect, it is interesting to note that the attitude towards words originally employed in non-mainstream varieties has evolved considerably over time. For instance, the first edition of the OED was largely based on the assumption of the existence of a Standard British English composed of words "whose 'Anglicity' is unquestioned" (Murray 1884: xvii). However, unlike popular belief, the first edition also included words of non-British origin, especially thanks to the efforts made by the then editor, James Murray, and despite the criticism received at the time (Ogilvie 2012). Subsequently, Burchfield's supplement appeared in the 1980s, and led to the 1989 edition of the dictionary, which was still largely incomplete as regards World English terms despite the international reach of the volume. Conversely, more recent updates have taken considerable steps towards a more comprehensive coverage of varieties of English spoken throughout the world.

It should be pointed out that some specific varieties of English have undergone a process of lexicographic standardization and, over the years, dictionaries focusing on various varieties of English have gradually developed. After *An American Dictionary of the English Language* (1828) by Webster, which was followed by dialect dictionaries (e.g. Cassidy 1985), several variety dictionaries have appeared. For instance, dictionaries of Canadian English include Avis (1967) and Barber (1999). The first comprehensive Australian dictionary was the *Macquarie Dictionary* (1981), followed by the *Australian National Dictionary* (Ramson 1988; Moore 2016). In 1997 *The Dictionary of New Zealand English* was published. As regards Indian English, the first significant work was by Whitworth, who published *An Anglo-Indian Dictionary* in 1885.

South African English also has a long lexicographic tradition, which includes works by Pettman (1913), Branford (1987), and Silva (1998). There have been attempts to produce a *Dictionary of West African English*, but the project has remained incomplete (Banjo/Young 1982), demonstrating the complexities in conducting lexicographic work focusing on macrovarieties. However, a successful macrovarietal dictionary is represented by the *Dictionary of Caribbean English Usage* (Allsopp 1996). With reference to the Caribbean area, other resources are, for instance, the *Dictionary of Bahamian English* (1982) by Holm and Shilling, and the *Dictionary of Jamaican English* (2002) by Cassidy and Le Page.

On a practical note, without neglecting the crucial influence of lexicographic authority on language use, Dolezal (2006: 698–699) notes that the "descriptive and explanatory adequacy of a dictionary does not in itself promote an attitude of legitimacy for the language being described". Thus, lexicographic work is considered as essential to evaluating the evolution of new lexical formations and their codification, but it will also be integrated with a broader perspective on language usage.

62 *Methodological approach*

5.4 Research approach

Figure 5.1 illustrates the geographical areas in which the varieties under scrutiny are predominantly employed.

As mentioned above, the eight varieties selected were investigated due to the use of ICE and GloWbE. South African English (SAE) is described on the basis of the GloWbE corpus and a preliminary version of the corresponding section in ICE. As, at the time of writing, this subcorpus is still under revision, and the sizes of its different parts are not fully compliant with the ICE conventions, any quantitative considerations have to be made after cautious normalization processes.[11]

The section regarding the language situation in Africa focuses on Nigerian English (NE), East African English (EAE) comprising Kenya and Tanzania, and South African English. The analysis of Asian varieties deals with the English varieties in Singapore, Hong Kong, the Philippines (PHE), and India. The following section is devoted to Caribbean varieties, with the Jamaican variety (JE) being chosen as an example. The choice to select pre-defined varieties heuristically allows us to conduct contrastive studies. However, such categories are not taken as atomistic entities observable in isolation, but rather they are constantly problematized and investigated in their reciprocal lights.

Indeed, in this work the theoretical approach to world varieties is substantially aterritorial. However, for practical reasons, geographical heterogeneity was one of the criteria used for the selection of the varieties to be investigated. Indeed, including varieties spoken predominantly in areas which are geographically distant allows us to discuss their reciprocal contaminations (or lack of) in terms of lexical innovation.

Although this study is inherently qualitative, the use of comparable corpora allows us to make quantitative comparisons where necessary and to

Figure 5.1 Varieties analyzed

Methodological approach 63

observe the presence of specific neologisms across different varieties. For any statistical reflection, data have been normalized to a million words and rounded to the nearest integer, unless otherwise specified.

The use of lexicographic resources in this work is fundamental to addressing some essential research questions such as:

- What are the main types on neologisms emerging in different World Englishes in terms of word formation?
- What are the functions of these neologisms?
- What neologisms, typical of a specific variety, enter mainstream ones and what implications does this process have?

In order to answer these questions, the neologisms emerging in a variety have been:

- tested for their presence in other varieties (especially through the use of the above-mentioned corpora)
- tested for their presence in specific variety dictionaries
- tested for their presence in standard variety dictionaries, such as Oxford English Dictionary Online,[12] Longman Dictionary of Contemporary English Online,[13] Merriam-Webster's Learner's Dictionary Online,[14] or Cambridge English Dictionary Online,[15] *inter alia*
- discussed, when necessary, in terms of their morphological, semantic and pragmatic features.

Instead of delving into a quantitative analysis of all the neologisms detectable, given their potentially ephemeral nature, this study mainly draws on the recent literature for the identification of the most frequent neologisms and observes their functions and their evolution.

The word-formation processes identified for each variety suffer from the flaws that a selection of this type inevitably entails. However, attempts have been made to focus on those instances of word formations which can epitomize forms of lexical innovation, not only within a variety but also in terms of cross-fertilization.

The aim is to see to what extent neologisms coined in World Englishes have an endoproductive importance as they become part of the lexical repertoire of that variety. It is also to observe whether these formations have an exoproductive value and spread to other varieties, thus affecting the English lexicon at large. In this respect, this study also considers to what degree standard variety dictionaries identify those lemmas as belonging to a specific variety. It also aims to analyze other words which are not present in the selected dictionaries but which emerge in spoken or written texts thanks to the use of the corpora employed. Beyond the lexicographic works mentioned, other sources (e.g. etymological and diachronic ones) have also been consulted in order to verify if the word has not yet entered a dictionary or, alternatively, has disappeared from it because of its lack of usage.

The integration of specifically compiled corpora and the Internet has a tremendous potential for linguistic research with regard to the lexicographic study of varieties of English. Indeed, several corpora of specific varieties are available, although they are sometimes only partially representative. The use of Internet resources may also play a key role in lexicographic analysis; for example, the investigation of national top-level domains (e.g. .kh, .za, etc.) demonstrates that the level of correspondence with a specific variety is high (Cook/Brinton 2017). However, in this study, Internet resources have not been used for statistical comparison, but rather to derive qualitative considerations on the sociolinguistic usage of certain lexical units.

On a practical note, a potential limitation to a study of this type is clearly represented by the size of the corpora as it is realistic to assume that a vast number of neologisms may not be present in the texts consulted. Moreover, the nature of a neologism makes it so chronologically recent as to be excluded from the corpus, not because its statistical frequency is insignificant but because its diffusion started after the compilation of said corpus. Besides the interpretative aspect lying behind the identification of a neologism (see Section 3.3), attention must also be paid to typing mistakes, as well as to the transcription of slips of the tongue or mispronounced words.

Another problematic issue lies in the difficulty to clearly discern a nonce-formation from a *hapax legomenon*, meaning a word which appears only once in a text, a corpus, or a language. *Hapaxes* have been widely investigated to describe aspects such as vocabulary growth (Tweedie/Baayen 1998) and author identification (Holmes 1991). Obviously, as regards the empirical approach adopted in the analytical section of this work, the size of the corpora used (although significant, especially in the case of GloWbE) does not allow us to define a word occurring only once as an incontrovertible case of *hapax legomenon* without a deeper analysis.

It should, however, be remembered that the aim of this study is not to compile an exhaustive list of atomistic neologisms, and the related word-formation processes which contribute to the lexical innovation of English varieties, especially given their dynamic and elusive character (see Chapter 3). Rather, it purports to frame the nature and function of a selected number of new formations and to discuss them with a multi-perspective approach, including through morphological, structural, pragmatic, and socio-cultural observations. Indeed, the nature of the study is predominantly qualitative, and quantitative considerations are employed mainly for corroborating purposes. Frequencies can offer thought-provoking insights on the usage

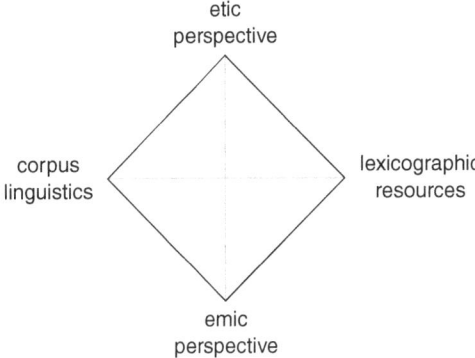

Figure 5.2 Methodological quadrangulation

of lexical items across varieties, but it is also fundamental to observe the concordances associated with such frequencies and to investigate their context of usage.

Thus, a fruitful methodological approach should integrate different tools and viewpoints, creating a quadrangulation which may be depicted as in Figure 5.2.

The method adopted is substantially based on a quadrangulation of approaches and perspectives, in which corpus linguistics tools are combined with lexicographic resources, and emic perspectives are integrated with etic ones. However, given the nature of this study, the emic perspective is not provided by ethnographic material collected *ad hoc*, but through the analysis of users' considerations included in the corpora analyzed. This orientation could be more widely developed in future studies using reflections offered by selected informants.

Notes

1 http://ice-corpora.net/ICE/INDEX.HTM
2 https://corpus.byu.edu/GloWbE
3 The South African subcorpus is currently under revision (see Section 6.1.3).
4 None of the excerpts presented in the analytical section (be they drawn from ICE, GloWbE or other sources) have been modified. They are all presented in their original form, despite any apparent inaccuracies.
5 SPICE-Ireland refers to a version of ICE-Ireland which has undergone a systems of pragmatic (SP) annotation to indicate aspects of pragmatics, discourse, and prosody.
6 See ICE outline (http://ice-corpora.net/ICE/design.htm).

66 *Methodological approach*

7   In brackets: number of 2,000-word texts in each category.
8   United States: US; Canada: CA; Great Britain: GB; Ireland: IE; Australia: AU; New Zealand: NZ; India: IN; Sri Lanka: LK; Pakistan: PK; Bangladesh: BD; Singapore: SG; Malaysia: MY; Philippines: PH; Hong Kong: HK; South Africa: SA; Nigeria: NG; Ghana: GH; Kenya: KE; Tanzania: TZ; Jamaica: JM.
9   Only the varieties included in the case studies presented (see Section 6) will be considered.
10 The lexical items mentioned in this section serve the sole purpose of illustrating the differences which exist between the two corpora in terms of frequencies. These lexemes will not be investigated here from a semantic or socio-lingual perspective. Selected items will be described in the related case studies.
11 I am indebted to Professor Bertus van Rooy from North-West University, South Africa, for sharing the current version of the South African subcorpus of ICE (not available for public download yet) for the purpose of this study.
12 www.oed.com
13 www.ldoceonline.com
14 http://learnersdictionary.com
15 http://dictionary.cambridge.org

Part 3

6 Case studies

Given the immense spread of English varieties around the globe, and their pervasive and mutable nature, this section can inevitably only present a restricted selection. Moreover, the exemplifying cases outlined here are not intended as comprehensive studies but rather as illustrative explorations in order to gain insights into particular lexical processes.

6.1 English in Africa

The principal African countries where English is recognized as an official language are as follows: Botswana, Burundi, Cameroon, Eritrea, Gambia, Ghana, Kenya, Lesotho, Liberia, Malawi, Mauritius, Namibia, Nigeria, Rwanda, Seychelles, Sierra Leone, Somaliland, South Africa, South Sudan, Sudan, Swaziland, Tanzania, Uganda, Zambia, and Zimbabwe.

McArthur (1999) distinguishes three different macroareas where English is spoken in Africa, namely:

1 West African English (spoken in particular in Cameroon, Gambia, Ghana, Nigeria, Sierra Leone, and Liberia)
2 East African English (covering Kenya, Tanzania, and Uganda, and to some extent Somalia, Sudan, and Rwanda)
3 Southern African English (adopted in Botswana, Lesotho, Malawi, Namibia, Swaziland, Zambia, Zimbabwe, and South Africa; see McArthur 1999: 13).

In light of the amount of vast geographical areas where English is spoken, and the heterogeneous types of communities involved, this analysis is restricted to three varieties. More specifically, the focus is on Nigerian English (NE) as an example of West African English, on the varieties spoken in Kenya and Tanzania as instances of East African English (EAE), and on South African English (SAE) as representative of Southern African English.

70 *Case studies*

Clearly, given the complexity which characterizes the language situation on the African continent, and the considerable differences that English assumes not only across countries but even at an intra-national level, this analysis does not aim to draw generalizable abstractions, but rather to investigate some concrete examples of 'lexical innovation' in selected cases.

Bokamba (1992: 135–137) discusses four main word-formation processes which are present in African varieties of English:

1   Semantic extension, e.g. *amount* (money) or *cash*; *bluff* (to give the impression of self-importance in an amusing way, or to dress ornately)
2   Semantic shifts, e.g. *bringing forth* (having babies); *minerals* (soft drinks)
3   Semantic transfer, e.g. *to see red* (a threat to harm or punish a person); *steer* (steering wheel)
4   Deliberate coinage, e.g. *the small room* (toilet); *nauseating* (homesick).

The following sections present a discussion of the processes mentioned by Bokamba (1992), as well as other formations, with a focus on selected varieties.

6.1.1 Nigerian English

The linguistic situation in Nigeria is highly intricate and it is estimated that more than 500 languages and dialects are spoken in the country.[1] The populace is growing at a fast rate: in 2010 the population numbered around 157 million and today it is approximately 186 million. The Nigerian Constitution defines English as the official language, while Yoruba, Igbo, and Hausa are considered as national languages.

English plays an important function as a neutral means of communication among the different local languages, and thus assumes the traits of a lingua franca. Clearly, this function has contributed to its diffusion throughout the country, and the majority of people can use some form of English or Pidgin English. Particularly problematic, however, is the distinction between Nigerian English, generally intended as the variety of English spoken in Nigeria, and Nigerian Pidgin English as a specific contact language.

More specifically, Nigerian English developed in the 17th and 18th centuries, primarily for commercial reasons, and assumed a major role after the unification of Nigeria in 1914 (see Alo/Mesthrie 2004; Adedimeji 2007), one which lasted until 1960. Nigerian Pidgin English (NPE) arose from the contact between English and local languages in the 17th century and has gradually assumed two main functions. Firstly, it works as a lingua franca which may be used as a means of communication between people

Case studies 71

speaking one of the many different languages. Secondly, unlike the so-called Standard English, it is also often considered as a means of preserving Nigerian identity. It is an interethnic lingua franca, which is largely recognized as demonstrating impartiality and neutrality.

NE and NPE are placed along a continuum of language forms ranging from standard to non-standard/popular/vernacular.[2] Diverse varieties may be used within the same community of practice, and even by the same speaker in different situational contexts, thus rendering the distinction particularly blurred.

From a socio-cultural perspective, it is also worth noting that various forms of NE and NPE are widely employed in Nigerian literature (see Chinua Achebe, Nobel Prize Laureate Wole Soyinka, or Ken Saro-Wiwa), music, drama, and cinema. For instance, songs by the Nigerian singer Fela Kuti represent a popular illustration of the use of NE.

As happens in the case of several WE, the definition of Nigerian English is controversial to some degree. Bokamba (1991, 1992) considers it a variety of "West African Vernacular English" (WAVE), while others more generally identify it as a form of "West African English" (Jibril 1982). Moreover, as Adedimeji (2007) notes, some scholars are not inclined to define NE as a separate variety but rather as a non-standard form of British English. Conversely, Odumuh (1993) recognizes the existence of a standard variety of NE as positioned within the area of new Englishes. Thus, it may be defined as an inter-regional and inter-ethnic variety of English which is employed both in speaking and writing, especially by the middle and upper classes, although Jowitt (1991: ix) points out that it is used by people with differing degrees of education.

The risk of becoming enmeshed in definitional disputes is tangible, but operationalizing the conception of NE adopted in this work is essential. Thus, it may be argued that NE refers to a variety of English largely used in the media, as well as in fields such as literature, education, and politics, across different ethnic and regional spectra.

As far as lexis is concerned, different categorizations of word-formation processes in NE have been offered over the years (see Alabi 2000 for a comprehensive review). In his analysis, Bamgbose (1982: 106–107) presents the following lexical processes:

- coinage of new lexical items from existing ones, e.g. *barb* from 'barber' and *invitee* from 'invite'[3]
- semantic shift: e.g. *corner* (a bend in the road) and *globe* (an electric bulb)
- preservation of archaic meanings: e.g. *station* (the town or city in which a person works)

72   Case studies

- modification of idioms: e.g. *to eat one's cake and have it* instead of 'to have one's cake and eat it'
- coinage of new idioms: e.g. *off-head* instead of 'offhand'.

This categorization may appear partial in that it does not take into account a host of other processes. Moreover, these phenomena at times appear to be overlapping and indiscernible.

An attempt to offer a more comprehensive typology is offered by Adegbija (1989: 171–175), who presents five principal processes:

- transfer, e.g. *outing* (a ceremony held in honour of a deceased person)
- analogy, e.g. *invitee*; *decampee* (analogically based on the other lexical items ending in the suffix *-ee*, e.g. *interviewee*)
- acronyms, e.g. *FEM* (Foreign Exchange Market)
- semantic shift, e.g. *chase* (to go after a woman with the intention of winning her love); *escort* (to see someone off)
- coinages or neologisms, e.g. *yellow fever* (Nigerian traffic wardens); *akara balls* (bean cake).

Although criticizable in some respects (for instance, the lack of problematization as regards the essentially interchangeable use of coinages and neologisms), this classification offers a suitable overview of the main processes of word formation in NE.

Another interpretation is provided by Bamiro (1994), who focuses, in particular, on the language used in novels and presents ten principal categories:

- loanshift, e.g. *branched* (called at, visited, stopped by)
- semantic underdifferentiation, e.g. *small boy* (little boy)
- lexico-semantic duplication and redundancy, e.g. *a stick of cigarette*
- ellipsis
- conversion
- clipping, e.g. *Perm Sec* (Permanent Secretary)
- acronyms/alphabetisms
- translation equivalents, e.g. *big men, bush meat*
- analogical creation
- coinages.

The limitations of the different categorizations and their unclear boundaries remain, however, evident. For instance, Bamgbose (1982: 106) classifies *invitee* as coinage, while Adegbija (1989: 172) includes it among analogies. Bamgbose (1982: 107) also identifies *bush meat* as coinage, whereas Adegbija (1989: 172–173) classifies it as transfer (see Alabi 2000).

Case studies   73

Adedimeji (2007) illustrates that neological formations generally derive from conversion, semantic change, abbreviation, and clipping, as well as from acronyms and initialisms. Affixation and blending, instead, are less present and it is hypothesized that this may derive from the fact that some Nigerian speakers lack a profound knowledge of the language mechanisms of English needed in order to activate these processes.

New words and expressions are often created to describe specific Nigerian linguo-cultural realities. In particular, words which are highly culture-specific, and for which an immediate translation is unavailable, may be borrowed from local languages. For instance, *oga* is an Igbo[4] word, which approximately translates as the word 'boss' and is found in the following example:

> Them go dey beg *oga*.
> ("Authority Stealing!", Fela Kuti)

Borrowing also pertains to several culinary words which derive from local languages. By means of an example, *akara* or *akara balls* refer to a typical Nigerian dish made of beans. The term *akara* in Kenyan English reaches a frequency of 1.71/million words, but the term is also present in Ghanaian English (0.41/million words). These data seem to confirm the linguo-cultural contamination emerging between African varieties, even beyond geographical proximity. This term also appears in other varieties, albeit sporadically.

> We have far too many market women, and not enough congresswomen, too many women frying and selling *akara*, and not enough chairing board meetings, close to 1/3 of our womenfolk occupy unspecialized roles.
> ("Women Affairs and National Development",
> *Daily Times Nigeria*, 15 August 2011)

> I encourage my children to *akara*, bean cake, moi moi and other affordable light food as noodles for breakfast.
> (GloWbE-GH)

The concept of *tokunbo* is also often present in its local form and refers to used cars of foreign origin.

> *Tokunbo* cars to cost more from January 1, 2015.
> (*Nigerian Eye*, 31 December 2014)

An expression such as *tokunbo car* is a representative example of how English and indigenous words may be combined to create specific compounds or collocations (see Adedimeji 2007).

74 *Case studies*

The three main regional languages of Nigeria (Yoruba, Igbo, and Hausa) significantly influence the lexicon of NE, especially in areas such as flora and fauna, traditions, food, religion, and daily life. In this respect, Ajani (2007) presents some examples which are encountered in a corpus of free speech (FP) or in Soyinka's *Collected Plays 2* (CP2), and the main fields which emerge are:

1   Music:

- *gangan* (a type of drum)
- *juju* (a type of music)
- *high life* (a type of traditional music typical of West Africa).

> Towards the end of this speech the sound of *gangan* drums is heard, coming from the side opposite the hut. A boy enters carrying a drum on each shoulder.
> (CP2: 152)

> *Silva*: Now, now, let's stop all this silliness. Here, let's have another go. It's all a matter of tempo, Chummy, not like *high life* or *juju* music. Now shall we try again? This time, follow the score.
> (CP2: 189)

2   Clothes:

- *agbada* (a type of suit)
- *danshiki* (a gown worn by men).

> A man in an elaborate *agbada* outfit, with long train and a cap is standing right, downstage, with a sheaf of notes in his hand.
> (CP2: 167)

3   Food, e.g. *akara, eba, egusi, tuwo, amala, ogbono, ewedu,* or *tuwo*. More specifically:

- *ogbono* (a type of sauce), as well as *egusi* (made from melon seeds), and *ewedu* (made from leafy vegetables)
- *dodo* (a fried plantain)
- *akara* (a pea or bean snack)
- *amala* (a dish made from yam flour)
- *eba* (a type of staple food made from cassava)
- *obokun* and *oku-eko* (types of fish)
- *ponmo* (cow hides)
- *buka* (refers to a cheap eating place).

> *Bola*:   What do you have on the menu today?
> *Waiter*:   We have *dodo, akara, amala, eba* and *tuwo*.
> *Bola*:   What about soup, what kind of soup do you have for today?

Waiter: We have *egusi soup, ewedu* and *ogbono*. Which one would you prefer? We also have bush meat, *obokun, oku-eko* and *ponmo*.
Bola: Okay, give me a plate of *amala, egusi soup* and bush meat. . . . How much will that be?
Waiter: Twenty naira and fifty kobo.

(FP)

The previous example also presents the terms *naira* and *kobo*, which are monetary units. These words, especially *naira* (the official currency), also occur in mainstream varieties of English and are often also detectable in the press, as shown below:

> The Nigerian *naira* plunged against the dollar yesterday after President Jonathan suspended the Governor of the central bank.
> ("Governor of Nigeria's Central Bank Suspended", *The Times*, Jerome Starkey, 21 February 2014)

4   Flora, e.g. *odan* (a type of tree which may assume mythical and symbolic values).

A clearing on the edge of the market, dominated by an immense *odan* tree. It is the village centre.

(CP2: 3)

5   Religion

   o   *Ogun* is the god of war and iron of the Yoruba people.

       Sidi: Is that the truth? Swear! Ask *Ogun* to strike you dead.
       Girl: *Ogun* strike me dead if I lie.

(CP2: 12)

The examples illustrated by Ajani (2007) also include cases of acronyms and initialisms, such as *PDP* (People's Democratic Party):

> Rivers Crisis: *PDP* Alarmed over Police Refusal to Arrest Speaker.
> (*Daily Times Nigeria*, 14 August 2013)

Another instance is *JAMB*, which stands for Joint Admission and Matriculation Board. By semantic extension, this word is now used to identify both the board and the examination itself.

Dupe: Bose, have you had your *JAMB* result yet?
Bose: Well, you don't want to hear it – although I made the cut-off mark for medicine, I was admitted to do microbiology at UI.

76 *Case studies*

> *Dupe*: Oh well, that's life, especially when you have no long leg. I learnt that Tola was admitted to study pharmacy, although she barely made the cut-off mark for pharmacy at Ife, and A.B.U was her first choice.
> *Bose*: I am not in the least surprised about that. Have you forgotten that her uncle works in the state governor's office?
>
> (FP)

The vocabulary of Nigerian English has undergone considerable expansion. As happens in other varieties, this is often determined by the inability of the English language to define special concepts related to Nigerian experiences and culture. In particular, semantic variation appears as a common phenomenon. As Kaan et al. (2013: 80) state, "semantic variation has been a pervasive characteristic of the Nigerian variety of English which has been cultivated and nativized to accommodate the culture and traditions of the people".

Semantic variation and lexico-semantic reinvestment are frequent in NE. The following passage offers some examples of forms of semantic change, for instance as regards the use of verbs, so that *chop* is used instead of 'eat':

> Them call you, make you come *chop*
> You *chop* small, you say you belly full
> You say you be gentleman
> You go hungry
> You go suffer
> You go quench
> Me I no be gentleman like that.
>
> ("Gentleman", Fela Kuti)[5]

In her analysis, Alabi (2000) focuses on five different types of lexico-semantic re-investment processes: shift, generalization, narrowing, re-assignment, and analogy. Similarly, semantic variation in NE has been described by Kaan et al. (2013) in terms of:

- semantic extension
- semantic narrowing
- semantic shift
- semantic reduplication.

Semantic extension is a common phenomenon in NE, and one which may be defined simply as "the addition of meanings to a standard English word" (Akindele/Adegbite 1992: 55). For example, *prophet* is a case of semantic extension in that, beyond the general meaning shared by mainstream varieties, in Nigeria (especially for Yoruba people) it is believed that a child who is born with long and thick hair is a prophet (Ajani 2007):

> *Jero*: I am a *Prophet*. A *prophet* by birth and by inclination [...] I was born a *Prophet*. My parents found that I was born with rather thick and long hair. It was said to come right down my eyes and down to my neck. For them, this was a certain sign that I was born a natural *prophet*.
>
> (CP2: 145)

Semantic extension also emerges in the use of family words which tend to cover a wider range of meanings. For instance, *father* and *mother* can be used to refer to an elderly person who is not necessarily a relative.[6]

Another case concerns the term *branch* which, as happens in the following excerpt, also means 'to call at' or 'to pay a visit' (Ajani 2007):

> *Tola* (to Kudi): Are we going to *branch* Dele's house on our way to the market?
> *Kudi*: No! We are too late already and mommy'll be getting worried about us.

Selected examples of extension listed by Kaan et al. (2013) are the following:

> I gave the police man *kola nut* before I was released.
>
> He has a *stranger* this evening.
>
> I *stayed* in Katsina for two years.
>
> Musa *hears* English language very well.

The terms in italics can maintain their original meaning but, in these cases, they extend it:

- *kola nut* (bribe)
- *stranger* (visitor)
- *stayed* (lived)
- *hears* (understands).

Words may also undergo semantic narrowing, as illustrated in the following instances (Kaan et al. 2013):

> Kerosene is more expensive than *fuel* (petrol).
>
> The family has a boy, now they are expecting a *baby* (baby girl).

The general meaning of these words has narrowed, and they now define something more specific, as happens in the case of *globe* when used to refer to an electric bulb. Another instance of narrowing is offered by Jowitt (1991: 254), who cites the lexeme *vendor*, which in Nigeria generally denotes a newspaper seller (although other meanings are possible).

It is worth noting that among the classifications available, generalization and narrowing are seen by Alabi (2000) as subcategories of semantic shift. Other instances of semantic shift are offered by Akindele and Adegbite (1992), who cite the sentence 'his *machine* broke down', where *machine* identifies a motorcycle. Similarly, *soup* may be seen as having undergone a semantic shift in relation to the term used in other English varieties, in that it refers to a side dish and is not generally eaten alone.

Semantic reduplication is intended by Kaan et al. (2012) as the repetition of the same idea. Examples found in GloWbE are illustrated below and may also be observed in terms of their tautological functions:

- *to raise up his/her hand*
- *to reverse back*
- *on sabbatical leave*
- *to return back.*

Tautological formations are extensively used in this variety (Kperogi 2015: 62–63). However, such forms are by no means exclusive to NE. For instance, the expression *to return back* appears in all the subcorpora in GloWbE and in some cases (Pakistan English, INE, SGE) its frequency is actually higher than in Nigerian English.[7] The fact that it also occurs in the so-called 'native' varieties also poses questions about its presupposed deviance from standard lexicon.

On a final note, Adegbija (2004: 23–29) describes different types of domestication dynamics of NE, namely lexical, idiomatical, phonological, grammatical/syntactic, pragmatic/cultural, and semantic, and emphasizes the need to make a distinction between lexical and idiomatic processes. Similarly, Adeyanju (2009: 11–18) stresses the importance of distinguishing idiomatic variation from general lexical variation. In particular, the scholar mentions and lists a series of idiomatic expressions used in NE. Some of the ones considered to be relatively new are (see Adeyanju 2009: 15–16):

- *Toronto* (probably fake)
- *letter bomb* (a heartbreaking piece of news)
- *Rambo convoy* (a gang of armed robbers)
- *to be wade* (to be full of)

- *aso rock* (an impenetrable building)
- *maradona* (a dribbler or a deceiver)
- *woman wrapper* (someone who is exaggeratedly fond of women).

Alo (2004: 73) analyses the semantic variation process affecting the word 'head'. Following the usage of *ori* in Yoruba language, the word may assume a vast range of meanings, as emerges from the following examples:

> His *head* is not correct.
>
> By my *head*, I beg you.
>
> ... if you have 20 million naira and you don't know how to run your company from there, then your *head* is not correct.
> (GloWbE-NG)

'Your head is not correct' is a way of describing someone as a fool. Consequently, in this case we may talk about a form of semantic variation, deriving from an idiomatic calque.

Another class of NE word formations is defined by Owolabi (2012: 49–50) as "deliberate satirical neologisms" and includes lexemes such as:

- *militician* (former soldier venturing into civil governance)
- *politrickcian* (deceitful politician)
- *executhief* (dishonest and greedy executive).

Examples of this type are found in GloWbE:

> No questions are asked as to how the *executhief* has spent what was initially appropriated. What a shame!
> (GloWbE-NG)

They can be conceived as creative forms of blending and are especially used in political reporting.

In summary, it can be argued that this brief analysis contributes to the illustration, from a lexical perspective, of the creative potential of a regional variety such as Nigerian English. Along the same lines, Adegbija (2004) states that the speakers of NE, in response to specific sociolinguistic stimuli, are carrying out a process of domestication of the English language, creating new lexemes which are not generally present in other varieties. Furthermore, these new lexical creations can then, in turn, spread to other varieties (neighboring or otherwise), becoming part of a repertoire which is constantly being enlarged and enriched.

6.1.2 East Africa

The East African region is characterized by considerable linguistic diversity (Simango 2006) and is generally described as the area which includes Kenya, Tanzania, and Uganda. Both ICE and GloWbE, however, only include Kenya and Tanzania as subcorpora. This is due primarily to the complex political situation in Uganda, which has made it problematic to obtain a significant amount of data (Schneider 2007: 189), although some interesting studies have recently been conducted on this variety (e.g. Isingoma 2014; Meierkord et al. 2016).

Conceptually, Buregeya (2006: 200) defines East African English (EAE)[8] as a distinct variety, and underlines that the forms of English spoken in Kenya and Tanzania display considerable similarity. In both countries, English is generally used as an official, second language and it is, thus, more frequent in written and formal contexts. However, some significant differences exist as regards the language situation in the two countries. In Tanzania the use of Kiswahili is predominant, whereas in Kenya it is possible to consider a trifocal hierarchy (Abdulaziz 1991), which implies the coexistence of English (especially in formal and official situations), Kiswahili (used as a sort of intra-national lingua franca), and a series of African languages (e.g. Luyha, Luo, Kikuyu, Coastal Kiswahili).

EAE at large presents several loanwords, especially from Kiswahili, and some of these words are often described as part of the lexical repertoire of other varieties, as in the case of *askari* (guard) and *bwana* (mister). However, results based on the GloWbE corpus illustrate that these words occur only sporadically outside the EAE region. In particular, Table 6.1 shows the frequency of *bwana* across the corpus.

Other loanwords are generally considered as restricted to the East African region, and especially to Kenya, such as *uhuru* (independence) and *harambee* (pulling together) which have become national slogans there (Schmied 2006: 195).

Table 6.2 shows that *uhuru* is predominantly present in Kenyan English (KEE), followed by Tanzanian English (TZE), which confirms the strong linguistic relationship between the two countries. In this respect, Schmied (2004: 253) stresses that, although a lexeme may refer explicitly to Tanzanian or Kenyan cultural elements, it is generally understood by speakers of both countries.

Table 6.1 Frequency of *bwana* in GloWbE

Variety	Frequency (per mln words)
US	0.05
CA	0.02
GB	0.03
IE	0.01
AU	0.02
NZ	0.01
IN	0.02
LK	0.02
PK	–
BD	0.03
SG	–
MY	–
PH	–
HK	0.02
SA	0.18
NG	–
GH	0.10
KE	6.28
TZ	4.49
JM	0.13

However, especially with regard to loanwords, some words are specifically considered as Kenyanisms. A selection of the loanwords in KEE listed by Budohoska (2014) is:

- *wananchi* (citizens)
- *matatu* (minibus)
- *orkoiyot* (king)
- *harambee* (all together)
- *jua kali* (literally 'hot sun'. It refers to craftwork and is also used to indicate people who conduct their business in open spaces.).

In Kenya the co-presence of tribal languages with Kiswahili and English inevitably leads to reciprocal influences from a lexical perspective. For instance, the word *matatu* is generally labeled as a Kenyanism, which can be found in the following excerpt:

82 *Case studies*

Table 6.2 Frequency of *uhuru* in GloWbE

Variety	Frequency (per mln words)
US	0.06
CA	0.01
GB	0.12
IE	0.06
AU	0.05
NZ	0.10
IN	0.03
LK	0.02
PK	0.08
BD	0.18
SG	–
MY	0.19
PH	0.25
HK	0.07
SA	1.10
NG	1.06
GH	2.76
KE	117.68
TZ	66.10
JM	2.83

Cities in motion: how we mapped the *matatus* of Nairobi. A project makes sense of the brightly coloured, seemingly anarchic minibuses that stitch the Kenyan capital together.

(*Guardian*, Jacqueline M. Klopp, 19 February 2014)

Another Kiswahili word present in KEE is *kitu kidogo*. Literally meaning 'something small', it is also often used to mean 'bribe':

... vote for Kanu, he will make sure that they get *kitu kidogo* (something small).

(W2E017K)

In GloWbE the expression *toa kitu kidogu* (to give something small) is found exclusively in the KE section:

It's evident that the cop want us to *toa kitu kidogo*, that's why he's got into the car so conveniently.

(GloWbE-KE B)

Another instance also appears in ICE-EA, in its Kenyan written section:

> while many policemen are disgracing themselves with their addiction to *Toa Kitu Kidogo* (TKK).
>
> (W2E011K)

Mitumba is an Africanism commonly used in eastern and central Africa, but it is often accompanied, both in speaking and in writing, by an explanation in English:

> Haji, a driver for a parastatal in the city says that *mitumba* (second hand clothes) are his saviour.
>
> (W2B011T)

> ... they decided to mobilize these people and for them first they used uh these used clothes *mitumba*.
>
> (S1B041T)

Beyond borrowing, another word-formation process taking place in EAE is that of semantic extension. For instance, as also happens in NE, words such as *brother* and *sister* undergo a type of extension and include people who do not have a biological link with the speaker.

As regards derivation, the main processes in KEE are (Budohoska 2014: 135):

- prefixation (*pre-*, *ex-*, *inter-*, *self-*)
- suffixation (*-er*, *-or*, *-dom*, *-ness*, *-ment*, *-(i)ty*, *-(i)fication*, *-ise/ize*, *-able*, *-(i)al*, *-ant*, *-ory*, *-ive*, *-ly*).

An example of prefixation is in the term *prewedding*:

> Yes, *prewedding* was on 30.8.91.
>
> (S1BCE05K)

Prewedding generally refers to the day in which, in some Kenyan tribes, a dowry is paid before the actual wedding. In GloWbE it occurs mainly in KEE (0.07/million words) and in TZE (0.03/million words).

Another example of this type of derivation is *interbetween*:

> I think uh there is an *interbetween* position between the adolescence and the childhood and that is the stage we call puberty and it starts with the physical changes that we see in a child.
>
> (S1B048K)

84 *Case studies*

This passage also shows a word-class change as *interbetween* is used as an adjective.

An instance of derivation with suffixation is found below:

> Such chemicals include pesticides, herbicides and fertiliser, while the machinery includes tractors, *harvestors* and harrows.
>
> (W2B035K)

The term *harvestor* is probably a different realization of 'harvester' (derived from the stem 'harvest' and the agentive suffix -*er*).

Another suffix present in derivational processes is -*dom*, as happens in the case of *tribedom*, which refers to the reign of a tribe:

> The latest to affirm that he remains devoted to those who would like to see this country split into *tribedoms* is Sharif Nassir.
>
> (W2E013K)

A similar example is *dissolutionment*, in which the suffix -*ment* is added to 'dissolution', creating a new formation which, semantically, represents a synonym of 'dissolution'.

To conclude, we can argue that the notion of EAE can be placed within the transnational context, which characterizes English at large, but it also specifically transcends national boundaries within the macroregion. In this regard, Svartvik and Leech (2016: 125) aptly state that "regional varieties of the language, sharing some characteristics with the local languages, tend to develop their own prestige values, and some kind of standardization – or convergence of local varieties – begins to take place".

Some lexical features continue to be characteristic of the English spoken in this area but, at the same time, others display a more evident cross-fertilization potential, which goes far beyond established geographical borders and can become a multicultural resource. On a practical note, further studies focusing on EAE should be supplemented by data drawn from the Ugandan English variety in order to perform a more comprehensive investigation of the vibrant dynamics developing within this macrovariety.

6.1.3 South Africa

South African English (SAE) intuitively refers to the English variety spoken in South Africa. However, as with other such labels used in the field, it also evidently suffers from uncertainty of reference, as the juggernaut of SAE inexorably grows and is characterized by diversity and complexity.[9]

Indeed, the linguistic ecology of South Africa has often been defined as one the most complex from a sociolinguistic perspective (Schneider 2007; van Rooy/Terblanche 2010). McArthur's vivid 1999 description of the intricateness of SAE is still applicable and manages to depict both its uniqueness and its strong relationship with a series of other Englishes in the world:

> It resembles the UK in the core ethnicity of its Anglophones and aspects of its traditional standard speech and writing; it is like the US in having a history of racial tension and kinds of 'black' and 'white' English; it shares with Canada a bicolonial history, resulting in a tense relationship between two settler communities, English and French in Canada, English and Dutch-to-Afrikaans in South Africa; it is like Australia and New Zealand in aspects of its southern-hemisphere English usage and in degrees of tension with the longer-established peoples of the three territories and their languages – but on a much larger scale. And finally it has also shared a great deal with settler communities that were formerly well established especially in Kenya and in Zambia and Zimbabwe.
> (McArthur 1999: 13)

White South African English (WSAE) in its acrolectal variety was generally considered to be the standard form until the end of apartheid (Bowerman 2004). Over the years, however, awareness has grown that the English spoken in South Africa is far from uniform, and Black South African English (BSAE) has started to receive considerable attention as well (e.g. Makalela 2007; van Rooy 2006, 2010; van Rooy/Terblanche 2010).

This section limits itself to some lexical considerations drawing specifically on van Rooy and Terblanche (2010), with a focus on neological formations and without aiming to delve into the tortuous peculiarities of the numerous varieties present in the country. Van Rooy and Terblanche (2010) analyze a corpus of 703,329 words from the *Vaal Weekly* newspaper with the objective of offering a detailed picture of neological forms and word-formation mechanisms. In order to investigate their level of acceptance, dictionary codification is one of the criteria adopted. In particular, the *South African Concise Oxford Dictionary* (SACOD 2002) is employed to this end.

The main word-formation processes emerging, and the related semantic domains, are summarized in Table 6.3.

One of the semantic areas in which neological formation appears significant is that related to politics. Codified neologisms[10] are, for instance, loanwords such as *amandla*, *apartheid*, *boere*, and *toyi-toying*, while some of the forms which are not codified yet are *Africanness*, *cadreship*, *deployees*, and *whippery*.

86 Case studies

Table 6.3 Neologisms in SAE (adapted from van Rooy/Terblanche 2010: 363)

Semantic domain	New forms	Not in the dictionary	Word-formation process (of forms not in the dictionary)
Politics	15	7	7 derivations
Savings	3	2	2 derivations
Crime/violence	9	2	2 compounds
Health	3	2	2 derivations
Culture	4	1	1 compound
Entertainment	7	3	2 compounds 1 loanword
Sport	6	6	6 compounds
Food	7	1	1 compound

A term related to the area of savings is *stockvel*,[11] which is present in the SACOD, while derivations such as *stokveller* are not. New terms are also found in the area of violence and crime, especially regarding specific lexemes to denote people and activities, such as *tsotsi*,[12] *gangsta, gangsterism* (included in the SACOD 2002) and *thuggery* (not a dictionary lemma). Other words related to specific instruments, such as *pangas* and *sjamboks*, derive from East African and Afrikaans words (van Rooy/Terblanche 2010: 364–365):

'Gangsters' with *pangas* storm school.
(*Iol News*, 24 July 2015)

No place for *sjambok* brutality in SA: DA.
(*Times* live, 10 November 2014)

Indeed, loanwords from the several local languages have long characterized SAE, and Afrikaans in particular has provided numerous terms. As Elmes stresses, "about half the words in the national lexicon that are distinctively South African originate in Afrikaans" (Elmes 2001: 85). Common are words such as *veld* (open country) and *dorp* (village), and they are now present in most standard English dictionaries, in some cases without being identified as South Africanisms, which indicates their spread and acceptance (at least from a lexicographic perspective) outside South African borders. Other words which derive from Afrikaans and which can be found in the SACOD include *tekkies* (trainers) or *bliksem* (beat up), and many other words related to the area of food, such as *ielie meal* (which also represents a hybrid compound). Other instances are listed below:

Case studies 87

- *beskuit* (dried hard rusks)
- *braai* (barbecue) and related terms such as *braaivleis* (grilled meat)
- *mealies* (ear of maize)
- *pap* (a maize porridge generally used in many African countries and the Caribbean)
- *boerewors* (a type of sausage)
- *sosaties* (a type of kebab)
- *naartjies* (a citrus fruit)
- *potjiekos* (a traditional stew).

However, many other African languages have contributed lexicon to the South African variety of English, e.g.:

- *khaya* (home) from Nguni languages
- *mampara* (idiot) from Sotho languages
- *indaba* (conference) from Zulu.

The numerous Indian communities living in South Africa have also provided words which originate from different languages spoken in the Indian subcontinent, such as Hindi, Tamil, Telagu, Gujarati, and Urdu. Examples include *brinjal* (eggplant), or *bunny chow* (a type of curry bread) (Esteves/Hurst 2009).

The corpus compiled by van Rooy and Terblanche (2010) also shows the presence of several compounds, e.g. *clotheswire*, *homegrown*, *spiderweb-wires*, *crossmember*, and *loadshedding*. The SACOD (2002) does not include these formations, except for the last two (spelt as *cross member* and *load-shedding*).

Affixation is frequently present in SAE. For instance, the negative prefix *un-* is used for terms such as *unchurched*, *unconcluded*, *unglorified*, *unroadworthy*, and *unsourced* (van Rooy/Terblanche 2010: 374).

Some of the words which traditionally belong to the SAE repertoire are also found in other varieties. For instance, the word *braai* has a significantly higher frequency in SAE, but also emerges in other varieties, as shown in Table 6.4.

These results, based on the GloWbE corpus, illustrate the frequency of *braai* per million words across varieties. Clearly, in most WE its usage is relatively sporadic, but its presence is significant as it confirms a potential contamination between varieties.

Interestingly, in 2015 the OED included three South Africanisms, namely *papsak*, *whoonga*, and *tenderpreneur*, which may be defined as follows:

- *papsak* (the foil container in which wine, especially of low quality, is sold)
- *whoonga* (the street drug alleged to contain anti-retroviral drugs)

88 *Case studies*

Table 6.4 Frequency of *braai* in GloWbE

Variety	Frequency (per mln words)
US	0.01
CA	0.07
GB	–
IE	0.06
AU	0.24
NZ	0.05
IN	0.09
LK	0.02
PK	0.04
BD	0.02
SG	0.05
MY	–
PH	0.02
HK	0.27
SA	23.74
NG	–
GH	0.08
KE	0.05
TZ	1.31
JM	0.08

- *tenderpreneur* (a blend of 'tender' and 'entrepreneur', used to refer to someone who exploits their influence in order to benefit from government contracts; this blend follows a pattern which has generated words such as *infopreneur* or *technopreneur*).

From this perspective, it should be pointed out that lexical items which are typically identified as SAE forms may spread to neighboring varieties and also become part of the lexical potential of the English language at large.

Thus, from a broader perspective, we can argue that the interstices and the intersections between globalization and glocalization constantly alter the linguistic landscape of SAE, especially with regard to its vocabulary. Deterritorialization and reterritorialization seem to be continuously evolving so that the definition of word formations tends to appear contingent rather than legitimate and, thus, need constant problematization.

6.2 Varieties in Asia

In Asia the main countries where English is *de jure* an official language are India, Pakistan, the Philippines, and Singapore. In other countries such

Case studies 89

as Bangladesh, Brunei, Malaysia, and Sri Lanka, English has, *de facto,* an official role and coexists with other tongues.

Given the vast diffusion of English in the Asian region, this analysis is circumscribed to four varieties spoken in a restricted number of geographical areas, namely Singapore, Hong Kong, the Philippines, and India. This choice is based on factors such as the number of speakers, the economic importance of the region, the status of the language, and its cross-fertilization potential from a lexical perspective.

Selected word-formation phenomena are described, and, given the strong bonds which exist between the varieties observed, contrastive considerations are also offered. For purely illustrative purposes, Table 6.5 shows some of the word-formation processes under investigation, with examples drawn from Philippine English (PHE) and Singaporean English (SGE)[13] (see Salazar 2014).

This schematization proves useful in illustrating the instability and volatility of varietal labels and the liminal borders existing between them.

Table 6.5 Word-formation processes in PHE and SGE (adapted from Salazar 2014: 106)

Word-formation process	*PHE*	*SGE*
Abbreviation	*CR* (comfort room, a toilet)	*CBD* (Central Business District)
Affixation	*Presidentiable* (a presidential candidate)	*Heaty* (hot)
Compounding	*Batchmate* (one who went to school the same year, or 'batch', as another person)	*Airflown* (transported by air, freshly imported)
Blending	*Fil-Am* (a Filipino-American)	*Singlish* (an informal variety of English spoken in Singapore)
Clipping	*Condo* (from condominium)	*Sabo* (from sabotage)
Conversion	Adjectival use of *traffic* (e.g., It's *traffic* in Manila during the Christmas season)	Adjectival use of *blur* (e.g., He is very *blur* and clumsy)
Loan translations	*Go down* (to get off a vehicle)	*Cooling* (cold, or of a yin nature)
Loan blends	*Sari-sari store* (a variety store)	*Ice kachang* (a dessert made with shaved ice)
Complete semantic change	*Salvage* (to summarily execute)	*Bungalow* (any detached house, even with multiple storys)

90 *Case studies*

Hence, some of the words represent instances of formation processes typical of a given variety. However, they are not etymologically, nor traditionally, linked exclusively to that variety. For instance, the word *condo* is generally associated with US English and the word *bungalow* derives from the Hindi word बंगला (*bangla*) although they are both widely used across different varieties. Thus, the fact that these words emerge in a given subcorpus does not automatically render them epitomes of a specific word-formation mechanism in a given variety. However, this table serves the purpose of exemplifying some of the processes selected.

6.2.1 Singapore

Singapore has four official languages: Mandarin Chinese, English, Malay, and Tamil. According to Bao (2005), the composition of the population has varied little since the end of colonialism, with the majority of the population being of Chinese origin and with the English language being used especially in political and economic contexts. English also works as a lingua franca in interethnic communication, a role previously played by Bazaar Malay and Hokkien (Lim/Foley 2004: 5–6).

The literature traditionally distinguishes between Standard Singapore English (SSGE) and Colloquial Singapore English (CSGE) (see Bao/Hong 2006 for an overview), where the former refers to the academic standard and the latter to the variety used as the vernacular, and both represent, in a way, the opposite poles of a continuum of Singapore English varieties. However, as will be shown, the concept of a continuum also needs to be problematized as it appears insufficient when required to portray the complexity of the relationships between the various forms of English used.

Singapore English (SGE) has also been defined as a contact language having English as its superstrate language and a series of local tongues (Chinese, Malay, and Tamil) as its substratum (Bao 2005). In this work, the concept of SGE has an inclusive nature and refers heuristically to the varieties of English employed in Singapore. Data are drawn from the related sections in ICE and GloWbE.

Although widely used, the term 'Singlish' is generally assigned a negative connotation or is adopted to refer merely to a colloquial form of Singapore English (Fong/Wee 2002). In 2000, the Speak Good English Movement was initiated with the aim of promoting the use of a more standard variety of English, cleansed of inaccuracies or unconventional traits (Rubdy 2001). On the other hand, the so-called Singlish variety is often depicted as a language whose peculiarities are to be maintained and preserved as they allow the enhancement of cultural uniqueness.

Case studies 91

In this respect, some speakers in the interactions analyzed offer revealing metalinguistic comments on the use of Singlish, and their perspectives diverge considerably. Some speakers neglect the existence of Singlish or the need for its theorization and equate it to a bad form of English, visibly assigning the word a negative connotation:

> Uhm firstly I like to say that I don't believe that there is such a thing as Singlish.
> (ICE-SIN:S1B-035#16:1:B)

> What you call Singlish I would call bad English because a term like don't shy uhm do you consider that Singlish or bad English.
> (ICE-SIN:S1B-035#17:1:B)

Others stress the importance of context when choosing which variety to adopt. Therefore, it is evident that speakers may switch from one variety to another according to the situational context:

> I totally agree that the use of Singlish has to be taken in whatever context me uhm and therefore uh when you say it's use in certain situations it's absolutely correct to use certain in a court I wouldn't say to the judge uh I wouldn't speak Singlish to the judge we have to use . . .
> (ICE-SIN:S1B-035#144:1:C)

Singaporean English presents diverse forms of lexical innovation, especially when mainstream varieties do not have an equivalent which is semantically satisfactory. As illustrated by Low and Brown (2005), some of the main processes are as follows:[14]

A Borrowing: represents the most frequent word-formation process in SGE. Lexical items generally come from Malay, Hokkien, and Tamil and belong to the following chief semantic categories:

   1 Food:
      - *durian* (tropical thorny fruit)
      - *mee goreng* (fried noodles generally spicy)
      - *rojak* (mixed salad in prawn paste sauce)
      - *teh tarik* (frothy milk tea).

   2 Culture and religion:
      - *kampong* (village or home town)
      - *bomoh* (medicine man with supernatural powers)
      - *surau* (place of prayer for Muslims).

3   Daily life, or description of character traits:
    - *kiasu* (fear of losing out, which motivates the behavior of aiming to get ahead, e.g. rushing for good deals)
    - *cheem* (deep and profound)
    - *siong* (injured, or used to refer to the immensity of a task assigned).

B   Compounding:
    - *shophouse* (a shop where the owners live upstairs)
    - *outstation* (referring to being overseas)
    - *neighbourhood school* (schools in the neighbourhood, usually less prestigious than *independent schools*).

C   Blending:
    - *distripark* (a distribution park or a warehouse complex).

D   Clipping:
    - *air-con* (for *air conditioner*)
    - *Taka* (referring to the shopping chain *Takashimaya*).

E   Back-formation:
    - *stinge* (from the adjective 'stingy').

F   Conversion:
    - *arrow* (to direct something, as in 'the boss likes to *arrow* the difficult tasks to me').

G   Acronyms: some refer, for instance, to the infrastructures of the country, such as *BKE* for Bukit Timah Expressway, *CTE* for Central Expressway, and *MRT* for Mass Rapid Transit. Others are also widespread, such as *MC* for medical certificate.

H   Derivation:
    - *kiasuism* (the noun form of *kiasu*. See Borrowing above).

I   New coinages:
    - *killer litter* (rubbish discarded from high-rises and which may kill someone by accident)
    - *ez-link card* (a stored-value cashcard which can be used for all forms of public transport)
    - *educators* (teaching assistants without a teaching certification).

Clearly, lexical resources in SGE derive from different language systems. As regards borrowings, several words coming from the Chinese language are present. For instance, a common term is *kiasu* (HKE 怕 *kia* fear; 输 *su* loss; Mand. *Pàshū)*, which is used to denote "a person governed by self-interest, typically manifesting as a selfish, grasping attitude arising from a fear of missing out on something" (OED 2015). This term is particularly frequent in the GloWbE corpus, also in compound forms which consist of *kiasu* as a predicate or as an adjective combined with another word. Examples are *kiasu kaypoh* (busybody), *kiasu philosophy*, or the structure *anti-kiasu*.

The term *kiasu* occurs especially in HKE (frequency: 3.77/million words) and Malaysian English (MYE) (2.71/million words). Instances are also found in other varieties, namely Canadian English, British English, Australian English, Sri Lankan English and HKE, but with a very low frequency (ranging from 0.01 to 0.05/million words). Interestingly, the GloWbE corpus also displays occurrences of nouns to denote the state of being *kiasu*, namely the composites originating with the suffixes *-ism* or *-ness*, i.e. *kiasuism* and *kiasuness*. However, such terms emerge exclusively in the HKE and MYE corpora (respectively with a frequency 0.42 and 0.05/million words for *kiasuism,* and 0.02 and 0.19/ million words for *kiasuness*). Remarkably, ODE (Oxforddictionaries.com) indexes *kiasu* as a 'SE Asian' term, MD (Macquarie Dictionary Online) and MMD (Macmillan Dictionary) respectively as 'Singaporean English colloquial' and 'Singapore English', while the majority of dictionaries do not assign a regional label (see the related discussion in Section 6.5).

Another word of Chinese origin is *kaypoh* (to denote a busybody), which does not appear in any of the major English dictionaries such as the Cambridge Online Dictionary, the Longman Dictionary of Contemporary English Online, and the Oxford English Dictionary Online. The same holds true for the term *gilah*, also spelled *gila*, to mean crazy or mad.

Culinary terms are often forms of borrowing, such as *roti prata* (a kind of pancake cooked on a grill), whose origin is related to Hindi.

After aerobics we go and eat *roti prata*.

(SIA-057.TXT)

Several words in SGE are borrowed from Malay, for example *rojak* and *kena* (to experience, to happen), or from Hokkien, for example *cheem* (profound, complicated), *chin chai* (carelessly, easy-going), *kaypo*, and *angmoh* (a common word meaning foreign, literally 'redhead').

The Malay influence on SGE from a lexical perspective has been investigated by Buang et al. (2008). One of the examples analyzed by the authors is

94 Case studies

Table 6.6 Usages of *makan* in CSGE (adapted from Buang et al. 2008: 10)

Meaning	Example (in CSGE)
to eat	Want to *makan*
siphoned	The money that Durai *makan* from NKF, no need to return ah?
food	There's *makan* there
taken advantage of	First day work sure kena *makaned* by lao jioss

the borrowing of *makan*, which may assume several meanings in Colloquial Singaporean English (CSGE), as illustrated in Table 6.6.

Among others, Buang et al. also cite the following examples as borrowings from Malay (Buang et al. 2008: 10):

I think the contractor *bedek u lah* . . . only 275A is completed. Next to be completed is 275D. [lie, bluff, trick (verb)]

Don't *pakat* against me [collaborate in secret, get into an alliance (verb)]

If I give up now, I *rugi* [make a loss (verb)]

I didn't want to buy a flat there, a bit *ulu* [remote (adjective)]

She just *suka-suka* change the date [freely (adverb)]

Other specific SGE words do not appear in corpora such as ICE and GloWbE and are not included in standard variety dictionaries (e.g. the OED). However, they emerge in the press, for example in the *Straits Times* articles,[15] as happens in the case of *remisier,* which refers to a Commissioned Dealer's Representative especially in both the Kuala Lumpur and Singapore Stock Exchanges:[16]

Remisier jailed, ordered to pay penalty for tax evasion.
(Elena Chong, *Straits Times*, 22 November 2012)

A comprehensive approach to SGE from a lexical perspective is given by Leimgruber (2011), who shows the presence of English terms which undergo a semantic variation and, thus, assume a different meaning from the original one. Indeed, some words "have been recombined to form lexical items with special local relevance" (Leimgruber 2011: 10). Examples are: *to take* and *to bathe* to indicate respectively 'to (like to) eat/drink' and 'to have a shower'.[17]

So we stood under the shower

Wah he got hit first you know then he jumped out you know.

And then we started like flexing ah waiting for the water pressure to go off uh then we go inside and *bathe*.

(ICE-SIN:S1A-082#128:1:B)

<O> slurp </O> Damn nice
Want some
Don't want
Eee I don't *take* beef
Why
I don't *take* beef means I don't *take* beef

(ICE-SIN:S1A-086#345:2:D)

Other word-formation processes can be detected. For instance, the ICE Singaporean corpus includes many acronyms and alphabetisms. An example of an acronym found in the corpus is the term *CISCO* (Commercial and Industrial Security Corporation):

Three *Cisco* officers hired by the clan were seen walking about.

(ICE-SIN:W2C-017#69:3)

Instances of initialisms are PIE (Pan-island Expressway), NIE (National Institute of Education), and SIA (Singapore Airlines), as can be seen from the following excerpt:

Hello I'm Shangi Barachargi I'm calling you from thirty-five thousand feet above South China Sea through celestial *SIA*'s new service for its passengers able to reach anywhere in the world.

(ICE-SIN:S1B-043#73:1:G)

Several acronyms and alphabetisms are highly culturally specific and often refer to the political situation, as in the case of *PAP* (People's Action Party) or *SDP* (Singapore Democratic Party).

I think in the past opposition grappled some of those concerns much better than the *PAP* but now the *PAP* has uh has taken the initiative on many of these issues that affect people's feelings and people's aspirations.

(ICE-SIN:S1B-021#51:1:B)

Compounds are also found in the SGE sections of ICE and GloWbE. Some of them are listed below:

- *wet market*[18] (a type of market selling mainly vegetables, fruit, and meat)
- *hawker centre* (refers to a cheap food center; see Deterding 2007: 76)
- *petrol kiosk* (this compound is only found in the Singaporean corpus, while other varieties use different terms such as petrol station or gas station).

> Where the *petrol kiosk* now stand was a kampong area and behind it a private garden.
> (ICE-SIN:S2B-027#65:1:A)

Compounds including the preposition *cum* are particularly common in Asian varieties (see also Sections 6.2.3 and 6.2.4) and also emerge in the SGE corpora analyzed. An example is *nature reserve-cum-adventure island*, found in the following passage:

> With the increasing need for nature-oriented activities in an affluent society and the world-wide trend in eco-tourism, there is a strong case for maintaining Pulau Ubin as a *nature reserve-cum-adventure island* to complement the intensive urbanised entertainment facilities provided on Sentosa.
> (ICE-SIN:W2A-029#4:1)

Other examples in the corpus include *monitoring cum control*,[19] *TV-cum-video machine*, *car-cum-driver*, *warehouses-cum-showrooms*, and *reading-cum-improvisation*:

> Mrs Fjeldstad recounts the case of a specialty carpet store in the US that was able to do away with its costly *warehouses-cum-showrooms* after installing several information kiosks in its 40-odd branches.
> (ICE-SIN:W2B-033#91:1)

> Art exhibitions are also part of The Necessary Stage's plans, besides starting a playwrights' programme, *reading-cum-improvisation* sessions with directors and writers to develop plays.
> (ICE-SIN:W2B-006#72:1)

Table 6.7 illustrates that forms with *cum* emerge across a vast array of varieties.

Table 6.7 Frequency of -cum- constructions in GloWbE

Variety	Frequency (per mln words)
PH	7.28
NG	7.25
MY	6.12
SG	5.65
GH	5.21
LK	4.89
IN	4.38
BD	3.65
JM	3.59
TZ	3.5
SA	3.37
KE	2.78
HK	1.95
US	1.93
PK	1.79
IE	1.47
AU	1.38
CA	1.37
GB	1.22
NZ	0.88

All the varieties considered present this construction, which, consequently, cannot be seen as the sole possession of any specific variety. The Asian region shows the highest frequency, with India being the country where it is most commonly used. However, as often described in the literature, SGE also includes a wide range of occurrences, for example:

- *founder-cum-president*
- *rap-cum-hip-hop*
- *editor-cum-writer*
- *yoga-cum-meditative experience*
- *chef-cum-owner*
- *bar-cum-restaurant*
- *bar-cum-club*
- *photographer-cum-birder*
- *leader-cum-deliveryman*
- *idol-cum-actress*
- *warrior-cum-military*
- *horror-cum-apocalypse*

- *shopping-cum-commercial centre*
- *tea-cum-ice cream salon*
- *dining room-cum-entertainment area*
- *tourism-cum-conservation projects*
- *conservation-cum-tourism programmes*
- *caps-cum-helmets*
- *exhibition-cum-talks*
- *sitcom-cum-spoof chat-show*
- *pool-cum-jacuzzis*
- *producer-cum-performer*
- *social-cum-gastronomic event*
- *biography-cum-confession.*

Clipping is also a recurrent word-formation process in SGE and the word *zomb* constitutes an interesting example:

> "once I get home I need a rest ... I just *zomb* out ... I don't read I don't do anything, I just either watch TV or just stare at the wall".
> (NIECSSE F19-f:26, cited in Deterding 2007: 77)

The lexeme *zombie* is shortened to *zomb*, but this may also be interpreted as a case of back-formation, or as a case of change of semantic category.

Another phenomenon which is generally considered typical of SGE is reduplication. Given the fact that both Malay and Chinese display reduplication patterns, it is not possible to define a single source of reduplication with certainty (Ansaldo 2004: 132–133). Reduplication assumes a variety of forms, such as nominal, adjectival, or verbal. Wee (2004) points out that nominal reduplication is often employed to express closeness or intimacy. By way of an example, in "Where is your *boy-boy*?" *boy-boy* refers to a boyfriend or a son (Wee 2004: 106). As regards adjectival reduplication, its use is generally linked to intensification. Thus, *big-big* equates to 'very big'. Verbal reduplication usually expresses attenuation or continuity. For instance, *stop-stop* means 'make a short stop' and *stare-stare-stare* equates to 'keep on staring' (Wee 2004).

Lexical items which are considered typical of specific WE varieties are continuously becoming lemmas of well-established dictionaries. As will be seen, this is particularly evident in the case of Asian varieties, including SGE. For instance, the OED 2016 update includes the following terms labeled as originating from SGE, and their lexicographic recognition seems to confirm their potential diffusion outside Singaporean borders:

- *ang moh* (a light-skinned person, Westerner)
- *blur* (ignorant, confused)

Case studies 99

- *chilli crab* (regional delicacy)
- *Chinese helicopter* (person who speaks little English)
- *hawker centre* (food market with individual vendors)
- *HDB* (public housing estate)
- *killer litter* (lethal falling rubbish, see above)
- *lepak* (to loiter aimlessly)
- *shiok* (cool, great)
- *sabo* (to harm, make trouble)
- *sabo king* (a troublemaker)
- *sotong* (squid or cuttlefish)
- *teh tarik* (sweet tea with milk)
- *wah* (an expression of delight).

Most of these items occur both in Singaporean and Malaysian English, confirming the strong lexical convergence between the two varieties. Examples referring to the expression *teh tarik* are shown below:

> I think a good cup of *Teh Tarik* should be strong, brisk and creamy.
> (GloWbE-SG)

> The drinks were of course, *teh tarik* for all of us.
> (GloWbE-MY)

From a wider sociolinguistic perspective, it should be pointed out that World Englishes are often characterized by the presence of code-mixing and code-switching, and the relationship existing between these processes and lexical borrowing is highly relevant to this study. These phenomena occur frequently in communities of practice where different languages coexist and may be used to fulfill specific needs in social practice. They are by no means exclusively representative of the SGE variety, but are discussed in this section for practical reasons as there is an abundance of revealing examples found in the SGE corpora, as will be shown.

Code-mixing and code-switching are generally placed under the label 'code change' or 'code alternation'. Whereas some scholars argue that in essence they refer to the same phenomenon (Clyne 1991), the traditional approach (see Wei 1998) considers code-switching to be a code change at or above the level of clause, whereas code-mixing refers to a change occurring below clause level. In this regard, it can be argued that the inter-sentential and intra-sentential levels at times overlap, and the two phenomena may coexist, rendering a clear-cut difference more obscure. However, for the sake of practicality, this work will follow the traditional distinction. In particular, code-mixing (intended as code change at the intra-sentential level) is often present in the corpus, as illustrated below:

100 *Case studies*

But home was also the discomfort of shared noises through the days and nights, looking out the window to look into your neighbour's window, and trying to do your homework on the floor with Chinese soap opera blasting nearby; it was looking after baby sister, running down to the coffee shop to buy *kopi-o* in Milk-maid tin cans for mother's *mahjong kaki* and walking up and down look-alike corridors selling *otah otah* or curry puffs and *nasi-lemak*.

(ICE-SIN:S1B-021#51:1:B)

Clearly, in this case English is predominantly used by the speaker, but it is combined with more locally specific words, which are difficult to translate without a slight semantic change.

This example also calls for a reflection on the need to problematize the link between code-mixing and borrowing. Although the two concepts are theoretically distinct, hermeneutic efforts are sometimes necessary in order to disambiguate borderline cases. In his work, Muysken (2000) presents a three-way classification of code-mixing phenomena at the sentence level, based on: 1) insertion, 2) alternation, and 3) congruent lexicalization. Firstly, borrowing can be considered as a type of insertion. Indeed, insertion refers to the incorporation of lexical elements or constituents from one language into the structure of another. For the sake of clarity, it should be pointed out that, instead, alternation concerns the switching between structures from different languages. It may happen at the boundary of a clause or involve a peripheral element (e.g. a discourse marker or a tag form). Hence, from a discourse perspective, alternation corresponds to a form of intersentential code-switching. Finally, congruent lexicalization is defined as "a situation where the two languages share a grammatical structure which can be filled lexically with elements from either language" (Muysken 2000: 6). Thus, it refers to the combination of lexical items from different inventories into a common grammatical structure.

6.2.2 Hong Kong

Hong Kong English (HKE) is gradually gaining international recognition as an independent variety (Evans 2011). A particularly important event for its codification was the publication of *A Dictionary of Hong Kong English: Words from the Fragrant Harbor* by Cummings and Wolf (2011), which set forth the process of lexicographic recognition of this variety, both from an empirical and a symbolic point of view.

In his 2015 study, Evans aims at assessing the representativeness of the HKE lexicon present in this dictionary by using diachronic language corpora compiled to this end.[20] The most common word-formation processes in HKE (in descending order) are listed by Evans (2015: 122) as:

1 Loanwords from Chinese (amounting to nearly 30%)
2 Loan translations (approximately 15%)
3 English compounds
4 Hybrids
5 Loanwords from other languages
6 Modified semantic reference
7 Prefixed compounds
8 Abbreviations
9 Total innovations
10 Modified grammatical forms
11 Preservation of 'archaic' usages.

From a diachronic perspective, the author also shows that, starting in the 1950s, there has been a considerable increase in the number of new formations, especially as regards loanwords from Chinese and loan translations (Evans 2015: 122). More specifically, borrowings (especially from Chinese) pertain predominately to the semantic areas illustrated in Table 6.8.

In recent years, several loan translations from Chinese have emerged. An instance is *silk-stocking milk tea*, tea made with a net-like filter, which appeared in 2007 (Evans 2015: 128).

The OED's March 2016 update[21] sees the inclusion of a number of words from HKE. There are loanwords from Cantonese, including *dai pai dong* ("a food stall") and *kaifong* ("a neighborhood association"), as well as formations in English which are only or chiefly used in Hong Kong, such as *sitting-out area* ("a small public space with seating in a built-up urban area").

The OED lists the following as HKE items present in the 2016 updates:[22]

Table 6.8 Examples of Chinese borrowings (adapted from Evans 2015: 126)

Area	Examples
Places	*Sai Kung*
Food	*char siu* (a type of roast pork); *bok choy* (a type of cabbage)
Chinese culture	*gung-ho* (spirited, enthusiastic); *kowtow* (to bow down on one's knees, submission)
Clothes	*cheongsam* (a traditional dress)
Games	*Mahjong* (a type of board game)

- *char siu*
- *compensated dating*
- *dai pai dong*
- *kaifong*
- *guanxi*
- *lucky money*
- *sandwich class*
- *milk tea*
- *shroff*
- *sitting-out area*
- *siu mei*
- *yum cha*
- *wet market*.

Clearly, many of these items are not used exclusively in HKE, but may be adopted in a wide range of varieties (with or without slight semantic variations). In some cases, a word may assume a specific semantic value in HKE, as in the case of *milk tea*, which refers to tea with condensed milk.

Table 6.9 Frequency of *guanxi* in GloWbE

Variety	Frequency (per mln words)
US	0.05
CA	0.01
GB	0.08
IE	0.07
AU	0.20
NZ	0.02
IN	0.01
LK	0.02
PK	–
BD	–
SG	0.40
MY	0.02
PH	0.05
HK	3.61
SA	–
NG	–
GH	–
KE	0.05
TZ	–
JM	0.03

Case studies 103

The term *guanxi* is marked as a HKE update, but the OED also states that it broadly refers to Chinese contexts. According to data drawn from GloWbE, its usage is clearly predominant in HKE, as can be seen in Table 6.9.

Other terms are also labeled as HKE updates although they are employed across different varieties, especially in the South-East Asian region, as in the case of *wet market*,[23] as demonstrated in Table 6.10 (see also Section 6.2.1).

The presence of HKE lemmas in diffuse and well-established lexicographic resources, such as the OED online, shows that terms specific to a given variety can become lexical items which are available to other varieties including 'native' ones. It also appears to demonstrate the cross-fertilization potential displayed by WE lexical repertoires.

6.2.3 The Philippines

While in the past Philippine English (PHE) was investigated predominantly as a sub-variety of American English, several recent studies have devoted special attention to this variety. This is not only due to the general WE

Table 6.10 Frequency of *wet market* in GloWbE

Variety	Frequency (per mln words)
US	0.04
CA	–
GB	0.01
IE	0.02
AU	0.03
NZ	0.02
IN	0.02
LK	0.06
PK	0.02
BD	–
SG	2.54
MY	1.63
PH	1.16
HK	2.52
SA	0.04
NG	–
GH	–
KE	–
TZ	–
JM	–

104 *Case studies*

research impetus, but also because of the awareness that the Philippines plays an important role within the language ecology of English in the world, especially in terms of numbers of speakers. Indeed, it is estimated that by 2050 the Philippines will have become one of the ten most highly populated countries globally, and this process will necessarily have central implications for the English language at large.

In particular, some works have investigated the creativity and diversity of the modern PHE lexicon (see Bautista 1997). As in other countries which were also subject to the English colonial presence, a considerable number of Philippine English words developed during the colonial era. Subsequently, other sets of words have emerged and have gradually started to typify this variety.

It should be noted that, in the past, lexicographic works were not particularly receptive to the lexical innovation processes taking place in the Philippines. In this regard, Bolton and Butler (2004: 91) state:

> despite the mechanisms of language contact and lexical innovation that characterize the creative, hybrid, and innovative cadences of contemporary Philippine English usage, thus far the major reference dictionaries, such as *Oxford English Dictionary* and the *Merriam-Webster*, have tended to institutionalize a petrified lexicon of Philippine vocabulary, evidently derived from an era of American anthropology concerned with the study and classification of the primitive other.

However, although lexicographic resources may still appear relatively static in comparison with the dynamism of the lexical repertoire developed in PHE, in recent years considerable efforts have been made to include new Philippine lexical items in some of the major reference dictionaries. In the last few decades, scholarly work has progressively started to focus on the PHE lexicon, and lexicographic materials have also addressed this variety more explicitly (see *Anvil-Macquarie Dictionary of Philippine English for High School*; Bautista/Butler 2000). Nowadays, PHE shows a great productive potential (Biermeier 2017), and Borlongan (2016) states that it can be placed at the beginning of endonormative stabilization within the Schneider dynamic model.

In its 2015 update the *Oxford English Dictionary* (OED) included a significant number of terms and expressions coming from Tagalog and Filipino usage of English.[24] The word-formation processes involved are several and include, *inter alia*, semantic variation, compounding, loanwords, and calques.

Some formations are hybrid in that they derive from the combination of different processes. For instance, *balikbayan box* denotes a parcel sent to the Philippines from another country, typically containing food or other products used in day-to-day life. It is, thus, a compound which includes a word borrowed from Tagalog (overseas Filipinos are known as *balikbayans*). Similarly, *buko juice* indicates a drink made from *buko*, the liquid found inside unripe coconuts, and a *sari-sari store* is a small store selling a variety of goods (in Tagalog the word *sari-sari* means 'variety'). Also, *bakya crowd* indicates a 'crowd from the lower socio-economic classes' (*bakya* are wooden clogs worn by peasants), and *common tao* refers to an ordinary Filipino (*tao* means human being).

Other examples of PHE words and expressions are *bahala na* and *utang na loob*. *Bahala na* is a shortening of *bahala na ang Diyos* (God will take care of it), borrowed from Tagalog to refer to an attitude of fatalistic acceptance. *Utang na loob* is an expression which indicates a specific trait of the culture of the Philippines, that of the sense of obligation to return a favor, a debt of one's internal dimension (*loob*). Also, the word *kuya* refers to an elder brother, although it is in more general use as a title or form of address used for an older man. As shown in Table 6.11, this term is predominantly used in the Philippines, but also sporadically emerges in other varieties.

Table 6.11 Frequency of *kuya* in GloWbE

Variety	Frequency (per mln words)
US	0.03
CA	0.02
GB	0.06
IE	–
AU	0.03
NZ	0.01
IN	–
LK	–
PK	–
BD	0.05
SG	0.07
MY	0.07
PH	8.30
HK	–
SA	–
NG	0.12
GH	–
KE	0.05
TZ	–
JM	0.05

106 *Case studies*

Other instances of word formations in PHE are described by Biermeier (2017). In particular, as regards compounds, Biermeier (2017) identifies coordinative compounds as a prolific class, which includes items such as *driver-bodyguard*, *back-carry* (to carry on one's back), and *micro-mini skirts* (very short skirts). An example of *driver-bodyguard* is found in ICE-PH:

> Witnesses say they often see the suspect picking someone up from school leading police to believe he is the *driver-bodyguard* of a De La Salle student.
>
> (ICE-PHI:S2B-013#)

This expression is not present in other varieties in the ICE corpus. In addition, GloWbE presents no instances of these terms in the PHE section and infrequent occurrences (statistically insignificant) in other varieties. Consequently, it is plausible to assume that assigning this word an exclusive PHE varietal label is to some extent a conceptual shortcoming.

In PHE, adjective compounds ending in -*free* are also commonly employed. Examples are *model-free*, *mineral-free*, *graft-free*, and *poverty-free*.

Synthetic compounds include: *chairholder*, *gunholder*, *healthchecker*, *home wrecker*, and *hold-upper* (someone who commits a hold-up or robbery). In particular, *healthchecker* is used to refer to someone who evaluates the risks and issues of a project. In GloWbE, this compound is spelled as *health checker*:

> you can get a free financial *health checker*.
>
> (GloWbE-PH)

Other compounds generally found in PHE include *junk fast food* (this pleonastic realization of the compound is not attested in the OED nor the Merriam-Webster's Learner's Dictionary Online) and *comfort room*, to mean toilet. This latter expression is present in some reference dictionaries such as MMD and labeled specifically as a Philippine English lemma.

Table 6.12 shows that this compound is particularly common in the PHE subcorpus. However, it can also be found in other varieties, such as Indian English and Malaysian English.

Well-known compounds in PHE make use of the word *jeepney* (a small bus), for example *jeepney strikes* or *jeepney drivers*. *Jeepney* is also employed in other varieties, although rarely, as shown in Table 6.13.

The compound *jeepney drivers* is found nearly exclusively in PHE (with only one occurrence in AUE), indicating that this compound has not yet been significantly adopted by other varieties.

Table 6.12 Frequency of *comfort room* in GloWbE

Variety	Frequency (per mln words)
US	0.01
CA	–
GB	0.01
IE	0.01
AU	–
NZ	–
IN	0.17
LK	0.02
PK	–
BD	–
SG	0.02
MY	0.17
PH	0.81
HK	–
SA	–
NG	0.02
GH	–
KE	–
TZ	0.03
JM	–

Combinations with *cum* (see also Section 6.2.1) are also present:[25] *affection cum friendship*, *non-formal livelihood cum literacy education programs*, *rice thresher-cum-dryer*, *cross-cum-shot*, *office-cum-store*, *tracker-cum-verifying*, *warlords-cum-politicians*, *shop-cum-subscription*, *spiritual-cum-political*, *producer-cum-director*, *professor-cum-architect*. However, as has been mentioned previously, this type of formation is amply diffused throughout the Asian continent, as well as other varieties. For instance, the expression *cross-cum-shot* emerges, although sporadically, also in PKE, BrE, AmE, GHE, KEE, and TZE.

The suffix *-ee*, which is commonly adopted to produce patient nouns, is also used in PHE to form new lexemes (see Biermeier 2017), such as:

- *integrees* (separatists integrated into the police force)
- *orientees* (a group of people orientated to a particular direction)
- *shiftee* (a student who has shifted to another degree program)
- *conveniencee* (people whose attention is taken for granted by other people called *conveniencers*, e.g. parents' attention by children or students' attention by mentors).

Case studies

Table 6.13 Frequency of *jeepney* in GloWbE

Variety	Frequency (per mln words)
US	0.01
CA	0.03
GB	0.01
IE	0.01
AU	0.06
NZ	0.06
IN	0.03
LK	–
PK	0.04
BD	0.10
SG	0.26
MY	0.26
PH	23.17
HK	0.27
SA	–
NG	–
GH	0.13
KE	–
TZ	–
JM	–

The frequency of the above-mentioned terms in the corpora is statistically insignificant and, thus, does not allow us to draw pertinent conclusions on their usage. However, with reference to the wide presence of *-ee* formations in PHE, Biermeier states that they may be linked to the American influence on the language as "the -ee suffix is more strongly linked to AmE" (2017: 38).

Another word-formation process emerging in PHE is that of semantic variation. One example is *advanced*, for a reference to a clock or watch which indicates a time ahead of the correct one.

The corpora also include the presence of acronyms, such as *KKB*, borrowed from Tagalog *KKB* (*Kaniya-kaniyang bayad*, literally 'each one pays their own'), used to indicate that the cost of a meal is to be shared.

Other more colloquial coinages are represented by terms such as *Imeldific* (extravagant like ex-First Lady Imelda Marcos) and *noynoying* (lazing around like Philippine President Benigno 'Noynoy' Aquino III) (see Pefianco Martin 2014).

> To this day, our energies are expended on uprooting the political culture of *Imeldific* consumption, sycophancy, nonaccountability, and greed.
> (GloWbE-PH)

Case studies 109

For me, the current administration is *noynoying* in the infrastructure and transportation projects.

(GloWbE-PH)

Such coinages are not highly frequent, but are revealing from a sociolinguistic, and even a socio-political, perspective.

6.2.4 India

With a population of nearly 1.35 billion (as of February 2018), India constitutes a complex linguistic mosaic. Reliable figures are hard to obtain, especially given the high number of languages spoken across the country, the varying status that they enjoy, and the intricate relationships existing between them. Moreover, in some cases it is not unproblematic to assign labels such as 'language' and 'dialect', and speakers themselves may not be entirely aware of these differences. It is impossible to offer indisputable data about the number of English speakers in the country and estimates range from 125 million to 350 million (see Lambert 2018: 1).

As happens with some other World Englishes, factual data are made notably difficult by the number of forms of English and the levels of proficiency present. The expression 'Standard Indian English' has been in use for decades (e.g. Quirk 1958: 13) to define the acrolectal variety of English within the lectal continuum. However, such a definition appears ambiguous from a sociolinguistic perspective, as does the general term Indian English (INE), which is somewhat controversial. According to some scholars, Indian English does not exist as it does not differ, at least in its written form, from other mainstream varieties of English (Krishnaswamy/Burde 1998). Other scholars emphasize that the expression 'Indian English' is inaccurate as we should, rather, be discussing Indian Englishes (Dasgupta 1993), considering the vast number of forms of English present. In this work, however, Indian English is used as an umbrella term to identify the English varieties spoken in India, as included in the related subcorpora in ICE and GloWbE.

Mehrotra states that INE "may broadly be defined as a non-native variety of English" (Mehrotra 1998: 15). However, the intricacy of the language distribution in the country calls for a reflection on this definition. It is true that only approximately 200,000 speakers define themselves as native English speakers (see Ethnologue[26]). However, some may argue that defining INE as a non-native variety is an oversimplification, given the heterogeneity of the levels of proficiency available. Indeed, Graddol (2010: 66) highlights that "English proficiency in India is distributed very unevenly across the various socio-economic groups". From a different

110 *Case studies*

but related perspective, John (2007: 4) also defines INE as a "cacophony of English".

In terms of lexis, INE displays several instances of lexemes which are considered typical of India or the Indian subcontinent. As will be shown, however, several of these words now also emerge in other varieties.

Some of the lexical items which are considered to epitomize INE are found, for example, in the area of food. An example is *brinjal*,[27] used to denote an aubergine. In some cases, this term is juxtaposed with its mainstream synonym in order to guarantee clarity.

> Of the soft ones, aubergines (*brinjals*) are the best.
> (ICE-IND:W2D-018#120:2)

The same term is also found, although less frequently, in other varieties (e.g. in Bangladesh, Malaysia, or Singapore), as shown in Table 6.14, and is now included in several dictionaries of English.

In INE, cases of semantic shift are also present. For example, the term *convent* may be used to specifically identify schools run by Christians:

Table 6.14 Frequency of *brinjal* in GloWbE

Variety	Frequency (per mln words)
US	–
CA	–
GB	0.02
IE	0.02
AU	0.02
NZ	0.01
IN	1.09
LK	0.60
PK	0.08
BD	0.73
SG	0.47
MY	0.62
PH	0.05
HK	0.15
SA	0.11
NG	0.07
GH	–
KE	0.02
TZ	–
JM	0.05

Today there are many nursery schools and *convents* started which give the education in the medium of English.
(ICE-IND:W1A-001#19:1)

As happens in other varieties, compounds made with the use of the Latin preposition *cum*[28] are also common in the Indian corpus, and Baumgardner (1998: 211) confirms that they are considerably more frequent in Asian varieties than in others (see Section 6.2.1).

That means the commercial theatre <,,> with their <,,> *music-cum-prose* <,,> scenery and spectacular elements <,,> on the stage <,,>.
(ICE-IND:S2B-031#5:1:A)[29]

Other examples found in the Indian corpus include:

- *diary-cum-memoir*
- *scientist-cum-politician*
- *train-cum-bus*
- *chairman-cum-managing-director*
- *fiscal-cum-economic subject*.

Some of the compounds described by Pingali (2009: 76–77) are:

- *auto-rickshaw* (a motorized three-wheeler)
- *table fan* (an electric fan meant to be placed on a table)
- *ceiling fan* (an electric fan meant to be fixed to the ceiling)
- *pedestal fan* (an electric fan mounted on a tall pedestal)
- *plate meal* (a meal with fixed portions of various items)
- *sacred thread* (strands of thread worn by Hindu men, with religious significance).

Most of these lexical items have emerged in particular throughout the Asian continent, and not exclusively in India. For instance, the analysis of the compound *auto-rickshaw* based on GloWbE shows that it occurs in 15 out of 22 varieties and its frequency per million words is higher in Bangladesh than in India (1.44 vs 0.58/million words).

It has been stated that compounding is particularly in use in INE even in cases where a compound is not used in other varieties. For example, Pingali (2009: 77–78) quotes *match box* as a typical compound commonly used in Indian English to refer both to a box of matches and to a box for matches. The analysis of the GloWbE material shows that this word displays a similar frequency in Pakistan and Kenya, and the investigation of this semantic difference is often impossible without taking into account the speaker's emic perspective, in that contextual data may be insufficient to be able to draw conclusions.

Some compounds present in colloquial INE are not formally accepted and are subject to social stigmatization, at least by speakers of so-called standard INE. Examples (taken from Pingali 2009: 79) include:

- *cousin-sister* (a female cousin)
- *cousin-brother* (a male cousin)
- *native place* (place of birth).

The first two lexemes appear so infrequently across GloWbE that any attempt to offer reliable statistical considerations would be inadequate. *Native place*, instead, is clearly predominant in INE, followed by other Asian varieties.

Other compounds are, for instance, *maidservant*, *wedding-blouse*, *meditation mate*, or *salwar-kameez*. The latter term is a coordinative compound noun (see Bauer/Huddleston 2002: 1648), in which neither of the constituents is English. It may also be described as an internationalism given its origin (Urdu). This word-formation process is based on the combination of two elements which are two garments (baggy pants and a tunic or shirt) and constitute an outfit typical of South and Central Asia. However, in GloWbE this compound is used almost exclusively in INE, whereas the term *salwar* appears across different varieties, especially in Asia. The compound is omitted from certain dictionaries (e.g. Longman Dictionary of Contemporary English Online) but has been included in others (e.g. Cambridge Online Dictionary). The OED includes the first constituent (*salwar*) but not the compound. This variation demonstrates the subjectivity of the interpretative process that lexemes necessarily undergo from a lexicographic perspective. INE also shows the presence of hybrid compounds consisting of a specifically Indian word (deriving from one of the local languages) and a standard English word. For example, *Hindipop* is used to denote the combination of Hindi and pop music; similarly, a *kirana store* denotes a grocery store (Pingali 2009: 80).

As far as synthetic compounds are concerned, it should be noted that *pickpocketer* coexists with *pickpoket* in ICE-IND, although the former is generally not found in standard dictionaries.

She has further alleged <,> that uh the accused <@> Mahesh Bakat </@> is a <,> uh *pick-pocketer* by profession and was arrested.
(ICE-IND:S2A-070#10:1:A)[30]

Following the common use of the suffix -*er* to denote an agent, *pickpocketer* seems to be limited to the Indian subcontinent. Although this synthetic compound (Plag 2003: 149) is a *hapax legomenon* in the corpus (with one occurrence in the HKE subcorpus), it is listed in Wiktionary[31] with a specification that it is predominantly Indian English. However, it does not appear in GloWbE-INE.

As regards affixation, a process typical of INE is cited by Pingali (2009: 81), who describes the use of -*ite* as a common suffix to indicate provenience. Thus, *Delhiite* means 'from Delhi' and *UPite* means 'from Uttar Pradesh'. Also a characteristic of INE is the use of -*wala* to indicate a person who is linked to a certain activity, for example (see Pingali 2009: 81):

- *paperwala* (newspaper and magazine vendor)
- *presswala* (journalist)
- *vegetablewala* (vegetable vendor).

GloWbE also includes other related examples, such as *designwala* and *rickshaw-wala:*

> if we are late on our way to college/office we are ready to pay *rickshaw-wala*.
>
> (GloWbE-INE)

Other processes, such as clippings and acronyms, can also be found in the INE corpora consulted, as in the case of, respectively, *non-veg* (although the expression is widespread in several varieties) and *BHU* (Benares Hindu University).

Beyond established borrowings such as *samosa* or *dhal*, other words which entered the OED in 2016 are:

- *aiyo* (expressive term which is close in meaning to 'Oh no!', or 'Oh dear!')
- *badmasha* (dishonest man)
- *bhelpuri* (popular Indian street food made of rice)
- *churidar* (type of trousers)
- *chutney* (spicy condiment used worldwide)
- *dhaba* (a roadside food stall or restaurant)
- *didi* (an older sister or older female cousin)
- *ghee* (a type of butter made from the milk of a buffalo or cow)
- *masala* (generic word of Urdu origin used to identify different mixtures of spices)
- *pukka* (genuine, excellent, and respectable)

114 *Case studies*

- *puri* (word of Sanskrit origin which denotes a round piece of deep-fried unleavened bread, served with meat or vegetables)
- *yaar* (friend, mate).

Although the words listed above are now considered to be stable formations in INE, they may assume the contours of neologisms when used in other varieties, as their codification in dictionaries does not necessarily equate with extensive usage. Thus, inter-varietal borrowings may be perceived as new formations for a speaker not acquainted with the INE variety.

Interestingly, a word such as *pukka* is cited in the OED as an INE term, but, according to the data derived from the GloWbE corpus, it appears more frequently in British English than in Indian English (0.21 vs 0.17/million words), thus showing its ample diffusion into mainstream varieties and the fluidity of varietal labels.

The September 2017 update of the *Oxford English Dictionary* led to the inclusion of as many as seventy words originating from INE, which were added to the approximately 900 INE words already present (Salazar 2017). The majority of the new lemmas entered the language in the 18th and early 19th centuries and so do not represent new formations within the INE variety. However, the fact that they have received extensive lexicographic recognition demonstrates their cross-fertilization potential.

The richness and the diversity of vocabulary is often achieved by the intermingling of different languages. Several words[32] are borrowed from Hindi (*bapu, chup*), Marathi (*vada*), Bengali (*didi*), Panjabi (*jhuggi, tappa*), Tamil (*anna*), and Urdu (*abba, gosht*). Some compounds such as *mirch masala* are given by words originating from different languages, namely *mirch*, (pepper in Hindi) and *masala* (which in Urdu refers to different types of ingredients or spices). Similarly, *dadagiri* derives from the Hindi word, *dada* which denotes an older brother or a leader, and *-giri*, which in Urdu combines with other words to refer to an activity. Thus, *dadagiri* refers to intimidating powers (Salazar 2017).

Other bilingual compounds are *chakka jam* and *gully cricket*. A *chakka jam* is the 'blocking of a road as a form of civilian protest' (deriving from *chakka*, Hindi for 'wheel', and *jam*), while *gully cricket* is a type of 'cricket played on the street', with *gully* being the Anglicized form of *galli*, a Hindi word meaning 'lane, alley, or mountain pass' (Salazar 2017). This kind of Anglicization process also shows the immense innovative potential lying in the lexicon of World Englishes.

Other new entries have been labeled as South Asian as they emerge across different countries, especially in the Indian subcontinent, and cannot be assigned exclusively the INE label (for a discussion of WE lexicographic labels see Section 6.5). These words include *bada din* (an important or significant day), *chacha* (uncle; also a respectful form of address to a man), *chhi-chhi* (expression indicating disgust), *gulab jamun* (a type of sweet fried in a sugar syrup), and *keema* (minced meat).

Thus, these brief reflections seem to confirm that the Indian historical and cultural background has determined a legacy of lexical innovations which continues to contribute to the enrichment of the English lexical repertoire, through diverse linguo-cultural resources.

6.3 Caribbean English

6.3.1 Contact languages and beyond

Before discussing Jamaican English, adopted as an example of an English variety spoken in the West Indies, it is worth offering some considerations on the importance of contact languages in the Caribbean region, as their development seems to corroborate once more the idea that languages cannot be easily caged behind rigid conceptual bars.

The Caribbean area is characterized by a heterogeneous cultural and linguistic composition. Among the several languages present English and Spanish are found, as well as French (the official language of Haiti, Guadeloupe, Martinique, St. Barthelemy, and St. Martin), and Dutch (the official language of Aruba, Bonaire, Curacao, Saba, St. Eustatius, and St. Maarten).

English is the official language of islands such as the Bahamas, Barbados, British Virgin Islands, Cayman Islands, Jamaica, Montserrat, St. Vincent and the Grenadines, Trinidad and Tobago, and the US Virgin Islands. In Puerto Rico both Spanish and English have an official status.

This linguistic mélange has brought with it the formation of pidgin and creole languages (see Section 2.4.3) which, as has been shown, are also characterized by considerable lexical creativity. Among the numerous creoles present in the area some have an official status, such as Haitian Creole (in Haiti) and Papiamento (which is the official language of Aruba, Curacao, and Bonaire).

In the Caribbean, different contact languages which have English as a lexifier exist. Some of the most famous Caribbean creoles are Jamaican Creole (JC), Bajan (used in Barbados), and Trinbagonian (spoken in Trinidad and Tobago). They may also coexist with other forms of English within the same area or community, creating a continuum of usage which is traditionally described as follows (despite the inherent necessary shortcomings):

- the acrolect: the standard used for official purposes, in many sectors of the government administration, and generally by the upper class

116 *Case studies*

- the mesolect: the intermediate variety which combines aspects of both the acrolect and the basilect
- the basilect: highly influenced by local languages and often seen as a vernacular form.

An extensive body of literature purports that these definitions are, to a large extent, artificial constructs which rarely fit multifarious linguistic situations. In this respect, many a scholar has highlighted that this continuum does not always develop linearly but can also be seen as an intricate network in which different varieties may coexist, and phenomena such as code-mixing and code-switching are also present (see Section 6.2.1).

Thus, this traditional idea of a continuum may be replaced by that of a complex matrix in which different forms of language reciprocally influence each other, coexist, and alternate according to multiple factors and forces (Saraceni 2015). Indeed, the concept of a continuum, despite its theoretical worth, may be limiting in that it shows a linear development which is not always detectable in real contexts. Contrariwise, a multidimensional interpretation appears more exhaustive in depicting the intricateness which characterizes the relationship between different language levels, as phenomena such as overlapping and alternation often emerge. In other words, even if we choose to heuristically adopt a more linear model, we should keep in mind that each of the language forms identifiable along the continuum is constitutively related to the others.

6.3.2 Jamaican English

As the investigation of all English-based pidgins and creoles spoken in the Caribbean would clearly go beyond the focus of this book, the linguistic situation in Jamaica is used as a case study which exemplifies some of the features of one of the English varieties present in the area.

Jamaican speech is characterized by extreme diversity and variation, to the extent that research has often demonstrated the inapplicability, in this region, of concepts such as diglossia (see Ferguson 1959, 1991), which is conceptually based on the coexistence of discretely differentiable languages (which are not always detectable in the Jamaican context of usage). In this respect, the notion of continuum has also been employed. For instance, DeCamp points out that there exists a "linguistic continuum, a continuous spectrum of speech varieties" (DeCamp 1971: 350). However, this notion also suffers from the inevitable conceptual flaws deriving from the complexity of depicting heterogeneous and cross-contaminating language forms (see Section 6.3.1).

Jamaican English[33] and Jamaican Creole[34] are typically defined as systems with their own ontologies and specific features. It would be inappropriate as well as futile to evaluate them in comparison with other standards of

English and, consequently, describe them as deficient in some respects. Moreover, the distinction between JE and JC is somehow ineffable. The English spoken in Jamaica may assume the traits of a variety of English, especially if we observe the acrolect. At the same time, it coexists, and is strictly interrelated, with a creole in which English constitutes the lexifier language and the West African substrate language is clearly present.

Using traditional distinctions, one can argue that Jamaican Creole, also referred to as patois or patwa, cohabits with various forms of English. In particular, the need to speak acrolectal varieties co-occurs with the desire to preserve basilectal creole as a way of enhancing an individual's identity traits. In this context, mesolectal forms are particularly widespread. With this in mind, it should be remembered that mesolects are not simply the unstructured and variable result of a combination of basilects and acrolects, but are instead clearly structured systems, which have flexible ways of integrating the linguistic aspects of other varieties. By and large, emphasis should be put on the discretionary value of these categories, whose use may lead to oversimplifications which hide the complexity of the linguistic dynamics emerging.

To some extent, considering the diastratic features of the different varieties, it could be argued that what is often seen in Jamaica is a type of gradual and relative varietal multiglossia. The two poles of the continuum may be seen as abstractions, which are inevitably influenced by the variety closer to those poles than those placed along the continuum. Thus, a clear-cut distinction between Standard Jamaican English, seen as a pure acrolectal form, and a basilectal creole is not possible as they develop along a line of microvariations.

For the sake of consistency, lexis is investigated here through observations of the Jamaican section of ICE and of GloWbE, and the term JE is broadly used to refer to the forms of English included therein. However, it should be pointed out that another important resource is available, the Corpus of Cyber-Jamaican (CCJ, Mair 2011), which is based on data drawn from www.jamaicans.com, in which Jamaican English and Jamaican Creole[35] are strictly intertwined.

The following passage is taken from a police interrogation present in ICE and clearly shows the juxtaposition and interconnection of different varieties in the same spoken exchange:

> *A.* When you went to the square that night and spoke to the police you did not tell the police that <@> Chris White </@> and two other men robbed you at any shop correct
> *B.* <indig> At di said time dem never tek up nuh statement dem just circle </indig>
> *A.* > I am not asking you if them took a statement or not.
> (ICE-JA:S1B-070#66:1:A)

118 *Case studies*

From a lexical perspective, it should be noted that JE includes specific compounds. For instance, the compound *wedding costume* is present exclusively in the ICE-JE corpus and not in other subcorpora in ICE.

> *Wedding costumes* are crisply laid out, bouquets and flowers delivered, wedding cars gleaming and decorated, catering arrange <l> ments finalized, beauticians have done their jobs, cakes are ready, wedding souvenirs selected, presents wrapped and about to be delivered. </p> <p>
> (ICE-JA:W2D-019#142:4; ICE-JA:W2D-019#143:4)

This compound may be used in other contexts, for example to describe a carnival costume representing a bride or a groom.

Another interesting formation is the coordinative compound noun *breeze-blow* (see Bauer/Huddleston 2002: 1648):

> If you make it through to the end of September and you haven't experienced a hurricane or at least a <quote> '*breeze-blow*' </quote> (which is the baby hurricane) then you can count yourself lucky & or unlucky.
> (ICE-JA:W2F-006#15:1)

This expression, which is closely linked to the Jamaican meteorological context, is explained by the speaker as a baby hurricane.

JE tends to use a significant number of polysemous words. As regards semantic extension, terms which generally refer to a member of the family, such as *father* and *mother*, are semantically extended to also indicate a friend or an acquaintance. As mentioned above, similar processes are also common in other varieties (see Section 6.1.1).

As far as the word-formation process of clipping is concerned, an example can be found in the lexeme *pickney*. It derives from *piccaninny* but has a different connotation, as *piccaninny* assumes an offensive racial overtone, while *pickney* broadly refers to a child. Examples are found in ICE-JA:

> All dis shame a little *pickney* like yuh bring down on yuh mother.
> (ICE-JA:W2F-018#174:1)

This term is now included in several dictionaries (such as ODE, where it is labeled as 'West Indian') and lexicographic resources usually mark it as 'West Indian' or 'Caribbean'. GloWbE data show that this lexeme is distinctive of the JE variety. Its frequency in the JE subcorpus is 10.66/million words, while its presence in the other subcorpora is statistically insignificant.

Another word generally indexed as JE is *yaardie* (or *yaadie*), which indicates a person of Jamaican origin. Outside the Caribbean, this term tends to refer specifically to a Jamaican criminal or gangster. This semantic difference emerges visibly from the excerpts below:

> Or if you're a *yardie* living abroad, come home and treat yourself to Jamaica!
> (GloWbE-JA)

> Secondly, you ignore the existence of racially-aligned criminal gangs that do exist in Western towns (*Yardies* for example).
> (GloWbE-GB)

The criminal connotation present in the BrE corpus is found, similarly, in the US one:

> You are a bad-boy *yardie*, and bad-boy *yardies* are supposed to know how to get rid of bodies.
> (GloWbE-US)

Within GloWbE, the spelling variation *yaadie* (phonological approximation) also occurs, but exclusively in the JE subcorpus:

> and you always run the risk of a *yaadie* not being welcome.
> (GloWbE-JA)

Indeed, etymologically, Jamaican expatriates would often define themselves as *yardies*, given that *yard* in Jamaican patwa means 'home' (Allsopp 2010). Correspondingly, the spelling variation *yaad* has led to the term *yaddie*.

Similar word-formation mechanisms emerge in *chargie* and *pawdie*, both referring to a close friend and created with the hypocoristic suffix *-ie*. However, these formations remain circumscribed to Jamaican Creole and are not diffused in acrolectal varieties of English. They both appear exclusively in the JE section of GloWbE. As regards *chargie*, only one example is found in GloWbE and the contextual information reveals that it refers specifically to song lyrics, thus in an artistic and creative context:

> "Mi parry, mi *pawdie*, mi *chargie*, mi one time linky," Deva Bratt deejays in the song.
> (GloWbE-JA)

Jamaican slang words are borrowed amply by varieties in neighboring countries. For instance, *gallis* (a lady's man) is found in Trinidadian slang, and *chichi-man* (to denote a male homosexual) is present in Belize

(Farquharson/Jones 2014: 124), alongside other terms such as *bashment* (big party or dance), *batty boy*, and *batty man* (also used to refer to a male homosexual) (Blench 2013).

Farquharson and Jones (2014) stress that Jamaican colloquial vocabulary is becoming very influential as regards modern slang, not only in the Caribbean area but throughout the world, especially among youngsters and thanks to the global diffusion of music genres such as dancehall. Thus, it is not mere speculation to affirm that, from a sociolinguistic perspective, word formations in Jamaican popular culture appear to contribute to the creation of new forms of cultural capital involving transnational and transcultural audiences.

6.4 Towards a macrovarietal approach?

For a study dealing with WE, the notion of macrovariety has central theoretical and practical implications. Ontologically, the dilemma regarding the intrinsic singularity or plurality of English remains to a large extent unresolved. Accordingly, a macrovariety can be intended as a single entity encompassing multifaceted forms (unified by a common denominator) and, at the same time, may also be considered as a heterogeneous group of single varieties sharing specific characteristics.

More specifically, macrovarieties are 'de-territorial'/'aterritorial' concepts, which display commonalities, as well as considerable structural differences. Conceptually, it may be argued that these differences render them, to some extent, ephemeral concepts. Macrovarieties can also be seen as post-geopolitical varieties, which represent, ultimately, dynamic processes rather than stable products.

Lexical production in an English macrovariety is sometimes labeled as the result of morphological processes which do not follow mainstream conventions. For instance, formations of words through affixation may be identified as regulation processes. However, the debate remains ongoing as to whether they should be simply considered as a deviant and erroneous realization, or as the beginning of a process which may lead to a more widespread use.[36]

It is nearly an axiomatic consideration that the idea of a macrovariety is based on simplification dynamics and the exclusion of culturally restricted terms.[37] This exclusion does not simply refer to the avoidance of specifically Anglo-Saxon idioms, but may be theoretically extended to mean a general tendency to use words which are perceived as transnational or international and lacking the cultural specificity which may impede understanding at an inter- or cross-cultural level.

Case studies 121

This consideration implies that, within a macrovariety, highly culturally specific terms (e.g. with specific national socio-cultural implications) may give way to lexemes which are more amply in line with the macrocultural aspects shared by the varietal compound. This aspect emerges evidently in the observation of a global variety such as ELF, but also within macroregions. For instance, if we assume the existence of a macrovariety such as South-East Asian English, we can encounter innovative word formations which are used across national borders (although with potential variation from a semantic or pragmatic perspective) but which do not emerge outside that macroregion.

In particular, South-East Asia is a vast area where the use of English presents interesting similarities. The strong economic, political, and cultural relationships between the countries of this region are confirmed by the presence of ASEAN (the Association of Southeast Asian Nations), which includes nations such as Myanmar, Brunei, Cambodia, Indonesia, Laos, Malaysia, the Philippines, Singapore, Thailand, Timor-Leste, and Vietnam. Clearly, ASEAN countries display considerable cultural and linguistic diversity, and it has been estimated that more than 1000 languages are spoken within this area. However, the role of English in this region is fundamental, to the extent that the ASEAN Charter[38] plainly states that 'the working language of ASEAN shall be English'. It may thus be argued that the linguistic features of the English language spoken in the different member countries show evident forms of convergence, but at the same time considerable differences continue to emerge, as the presence of a political organization does not equate to the presence of a single form of English.

From this perspective, the investigation of macrovarieties represents a potentially fruitful avenue for research, especially as regards their lexical developments. Indeed, as Salazar (2014: 104) purports, "little attention has been given to the comparative analysis of a set of national or regional varieties to determine whether certain words or phrases are exclusive to their variety of origin or shared by a number of different varieties".

In this regard, GloWbE represents a suitable tool to identify the presence of a lexical item across groups of varieties present in the corpus, allowing us to gain valuable comparative insights into WE. In this vein, Salazar (2014) observes the occurrence of a series of words across three different Asian varieties. The words are:

- *handphone* (a mobile phone)
- *makan* (food, eating)
- *siomai/siew mai* (traditional Chinese dumpling)
- *void deck* (vacant ground floor of a block of flats)
- *wet market* (market selling fresh meat and produce).

Table 6.15 Lexical items in PHE, SGE, and MYE (adapted from Salazar 2014: 105)

	PHE		SGE		MYE	
	Raw freq.	Freq.	Raw freq.	Freq.	Raw freq.	Freq.
handphone	3	0.07	196	4.56	170	4.08
makan	2	0.05	104	2.42	268	6.44
siomai /	85	19.71	11	0.26	0	0
siew mai	0	0	35	0.81	20	0.48
void deck	0	0	106	2.47	2	0.05
wet market	50	0.02	109	2.54	68	1.63

Data refer to Philippine, Singaporean and Malaysian English, and are based on the respective subcorpora in GloWbE. The words and expressions analyzed emerge across the three varieties with different frequencies, as illustrated in Table 6.15.

In many cases, it would be misleading to label a lexical item as belonging to one single variety exclusively. Nevertheless, lemmas of this type, when included in lexicographic resources, do not always show multiple regional origins, as will be illustrated in Section 6.5.

6.5 WE lexicographic labels

From a lexicographic perspective, in a constantly complexifying linguistic situation, the precision and incontrovertibility of lemmas which index a specific variety remains subject to vivid debate. Some may argue that the spread of lexical items across varieties and their reciprocal contamination makes clear-cut distinctions not only superfluous but even fallacious. On the other hand, such labels can offer thought-provoking sociolinguistic insights.

For instance, different varieties spoken in South-East Asia may use a common term which emerges throughout the macroregion, and when such a word enters a mainstream dictionary, the specification of a single regional variety may appear limiting. In this respect, the use of an overarching 'South-East Asian' label is also possible, but the decision to adopt it is always complex, especially if minor semantic differences or pragmatic nuances emerge among the varieties.

Table 6.16 presents an outline of some of the varietal lemmas found in a range of selected dictionaries[39] with the related varietal labels if present (adapted from Ooi 2018: 168). Only specific examples relevant to the varieties dealt with in this study are included.

Table 6.16 Dictionary 'labels' for WE lexical items

dict. / lemma	ODE	OALD	MW	CEDO	WW	CD	MD	MMD
blur[1]	SE Asian	–	–	–	–	–	Singaporean and Malaysian English colloquial	–
bungalow	SE Asia	in some Asian countries	US	–	–	in India / in American English	In India / In South-East Asia	British / American
handphone	SE Asian	–	–	–	–	–	–	Malaysian English
mabuhay	Philippine English	–	–	–	–	–	–	Philippine English Interjection
robot[2]	South African	South African English	–	South African English	S. African	South Africa	South African	South African informal
void deck	SE Asian	South East Asian English	–	–	–	–	Singaporean English	–

1 (adj) meaning stupid, confused, or confusing.
2 referring to traffic lights.

This table shows that lexical entries such as *robot*, meaning traffic lights, are generally labeled uniformly as a South African English word by most lexicographic resources.

In other cases, the attribution of a label is more complex. For instance, the word *bungalow*, commonly used throughout the world, is in some cases labeled as South-East Asian English, thus *de facto* recognizing the existence of a macrovariety of English in the region. Other resources (e.g. CD) restrict the attribution of this term to Indian English or American English, assigning slight changes in meaning (in INE it signifies a "one-storey house, usually surrounded by a veranda", while in American English it refers to "a small house or cottage, usually of one story and an attic"). Some resources do not seem to acknowledge the Asian origin of the term and label it as AmE. Finally, others do not assign any label, in light of the widespread diffusion that the term has reached.

Similarly, *handphone* lacks a varietal label in most cases, but is also identified as 'Malaysian English' (see MMD) or 'SE Asian' (see ODE); it is present especially across Asian varieties (see Sections 6.4 and 6.5), which demonstrates the ever-changing ebb and flow of the cross-contamination of varietal word stocks.

Greater efforts are increasingly being made to acknowledge the importance of the inclusion of WE lemmas in lexicographic materials. Such resources may provide diatopic or diastratic/diaglossical information, with varying degrees of specialization (e.g. Singaporean English, South-East Asian English, colloquial, slang), but such attributions at times appear inevitably static and inflexible. These labels are assigned during a complex editorial process, which should take into account both emic and etic perspectives (Ooi 2018: 174). This way, the insights offered by speakers themselves can be combined with an external standpoint in order to gain a more comprehensive view of lexical usage.

Moreover, processes such as globalization, migration, and online communication determine the impossibility of describing a variety as exclusive to a specific community (Ooi 2018: 179). Consequently, varietal labels should be constantly problematized, redefined, and challenged.

Notes

1 Source: Ethnologue (www.ethnologue.com/country/NG) (accessed 17/03/2018).
2 The concept of continuum is explored in more depth in Section 6.3.1.
3 These examples, following on from Chapter 4, refer more specifically to clipping and suffixation. However, according to Bamgbose (1982), they can be included in the macro-category of coinages from existing terms.
4 Igbo is spoken mainly in Southeast Nigeria and includes different Igboid dialects (Fardon/Furniss 1994: 66).

Case studies 125

5 From a more general perspective, one may note that other features which are typical of other English varieties, as well as pidgin and creole languages, may be found in this passage, such as: alternation of subject and object (me/I, They/them); infinitive forms used independently of the subject present (I be); 'go' used to express a future form.
6 As will be shown, this process is also present in other varieties (e.g. East African English).
7 These dynamics are also in line with lexical tendencies generally emerging in ELF.
8 East African English (EAE) can be interpreted as a transnational variety. This concept will be described in more detail in Section 6.4, where the notion of macrovariety is presented. In this study, East Africa is investigated adopting an inclusive approach embracing both Kenya and Tanzania, thus focusing on lexical innovation phenomena emerging in East Africa at large. However, cultural specificities will be accounted for when necessary.
9 For a historical discussion of South African English varieties and koinéization processes see Bekker 2012.
10 Given that the SACOD 2002 remains the most established lexicographic source for the South African variety, and no new edition has since been published, the data refer to the original study by van Rooy and Terblanche 2010.
11 *Stokvel* represents an 'adaptation of stock-fair resulting from a pronunciation mistakenly suggesting that the word is from Afrikaans, so named from the rotating cattle auctions held by English settlers in the 19th century' (SACOD 2002: 1155). It is also used to define a savings club.
12 *Tsotsi*: noun used to define a scheming character or a young black urban criminal. The expression has now entered mainstream varieties. Its origin is perhaps from Nguni *tsotsa*, which means 'to dress flashily'.
13 It should be pointed out that not all lexicographic resources assign the same labels to these entries (see Section 6.5).
14 Given their historical development, SGE and Malaysian English display considerable similarities, and most of the examples illustrated in this section are also employed in Malaysia.
15 Articles have been selected from issues during the period 2007–2017.
16 This word is French in origin but is now essentially limited to the Singapore and Kuala Lumpur Stock Exchanges.
17 It is worth noting that similar lexical phenomena are found across ELF.
18 This term is common to different Asian varieties of English (see Section 6.2.2).
19 Not hyphenated in the corpus.
20 The corpora compiled by Evans include:

- proceedings of the HK Legislative Council
- letters to leading HK English-language newspapers
- articles, letters, and interviews in magazines
- letters to the *South China Morning Post*
- Corpus of Global Web-based English.

21 OED (2016) "New Hong Kong English Words". Available at: http://public.oed.com/the-oed-today/recent-updates-to-the-oed/previous-updates/march-2016-update/new-hong-kong-english-words/ (accessed 06/12/2017).
22 Definitions are reported in Appendix 1 and are taken from the Oxford English Dictionary online. See www.oed.com (accessed 06/12/2017).

126 *Case studies*

23 The spelling *wetmarket* also appears once in SGE and twice in HKE, and consequently is not considered statistically significant.
24 A list of these terms is included in Appendix 2.
25 The expressions are presented as found in the corpus (hence with, and without, hyphens).
26 See www.ethnologue.com/country/IN/languages (accessed 21/02/2018).
27 Also present in SAE (see Section 6.1.3).
28 In this study, examples of this kind of compound are offered mainly for Singaporean, Philippine, and Indian varieties. However, it should be noted that this example also occurs in different geographical areas, such as Kenya, Tanzania, New Zealand, and Jamaica.
29 <,,> indicates a pause of between one and two seconds.
30 <,> indicates a pause of up to, or equal to, one second.
31 Wiktionary: https://en.wiktionary.org/wiki/pickpocketer (accessed 21/02/2018).
32 All the following examples are provided by Salazar (2017).
33 From a lexicographic perspective, an important contribution to the investigation of JE was offered by the first comprehensive dictionary of Jamaican English, Cassidy and Le Page's *Dictionary of Jamaican English*, which dates back to 1967.
34 For a description of the main morphological and syntactical traits of Jamaican Creole see Patrick 2004.
35 Methodologically, the study of Jamaican Creole may be particularly complex because of the lack of standardized orthography. However, the use of internet resources (as found in the Corpus of Cyber-Jamaican) is particularly valuable, for instance in studying stylistic differences.
36 This process is also evident in English as a Lingua Franca (see Mauranen 2012: 126). However, the notion of ELF as a macrovariety should also be more deeply problematized, but such discussion would go beyond the scope of this chapter.
37 See Seidlhofer (2004: 220) in relation to ELF.
38 See the ASEAN Charter, www.aseansec.org/21069.pdf (accessed 28/11/2017).
39 Abbreviations as follows:

    ODE   Oxforddictionaries.com
    OALD Oxford Advanced Learner's Dictionary Online
    MW   Merriam-Webster's Learner's Dictionary Online
    CEDO Cambridge English Dictionary Online
    WW   WorldWeb Online Dictionary
    CD   Collins English Dictionary (online)
    MD   Macquarie Dictionary Online
    MMD   Macmillan Dictionary (online)

7 Conclusions

This work arose from the intellectual fervor which has recently inspired scholars to explore the evolution of World Englishes together with the related paradigmatic shifts.

Despite the limitations of any categorization, it is apparent that WE are spreading, and some of them are now regarded as new reference models in certain communities and in specific educational contexts. Nevertheless, the aim of this study was not to set off on a quest for peculiarities in order to thoroughly define all the features which characterize each variety in its uniqueness. Instead, the fulcrum was the exploration of word-formation phenomena within a theoretical model which entails the possibility to view Englishes in a less atomistic way.

The crucial preliminary assumption is that the notions of 'varieties', 'English', and 'World Englishes' are remarkably fluid and conceptually insidious (see Chapter 2) and need constant problematization. More specifically, the Englishes analyzed have not been described as lesser-known varieties. Indeed, given that their preference of usage may be high and that their level of standardization varies, such a definition would be notably problematic if applied to the varieties explored in this work. Also, the approach adopted goes beyond a binary distinction between native and non-native varieties, as this dichotomy neither provides a theoretically scrupulous analytical tool nor serves a useful social purpose (Brutt-Griffler/ Samimy 2001: 105).

In particular, starting from a discussion of different types of word-formation processes, this work has investigated lexical innovation and cross-fertilization focusing on different WE. Thus, word formations originating within a variety (or traditionally associated with a certain variety) also represent items which can enrich other language worlds.

The ultimate scope was to observe how language as a social practice allows speakers to exploit a vast, fluid, and reciprocally contaminated repertoire of lexical and semiotic resources. Indeed, seeing varieties from a dynamic, ecological perspective means acknowledging that they impact one another with repercussions for the cultures they embody.

7.1 Evolving paradigms

From a lexical point of view, the fact that innovation processes are pervasive in World Englishes seems to demonstrate that regional varieties often undergo appropriation processes, which allow speakers to adapt the language to fit the local milieu in a creative way. Indeed, in several varieties of English, the lexicon presents significant peculiarities which make a specific variety unique. From a socio-historical perspective, this uniqueness is in line with the idea that a higher level of exclusivity may be seen as a way of neutralizing static conceptions of 'Standard' English (and the notion of Anglo-Saxon hegemony which it brings with it), while preserving its necessary usage. This form of appropriation is not necessarily associated with a subversive process which has an anti-imperialistic ethos. Rather, it is an inevitable sociolinguistic development.

However, these dynamics are fluid and circular, and similar processes can belong to different diastratic and diatopic varieties. Thus, the items produced can in turn become sources of appropriation by speakers of other varieties. This process undermines the possibility of assigning each variety a clear status, but it is one of the elements which contribute to the lexical diversity of Englishes. Rather than a limitation, it is, thus, simply a social fact, and potentially a source of enrichment.

The labyrinthine innovation processes which develop within the uniqueness of each variety, and the constant intertwining of different forms of English, tangibly demonstrate the "volatility of language borders", which brings with it the need to problematize the very concept of language (Saraceni 2015: 132). Thus, this study of WE is also pursuant to the idea of 'English Worlds', where the English language in all its forms is intended not only as a system but also as a world of usage, in which the emphasis is placed on practice (see Bolton 2013 on the concept of language worlds).

This work has shown that even though the expression World Englishes itself is well established in linguistics studies and may thus appear unproblematic, daily challenges are posed by the dynamic and evolving nature of this concept, which is based on shifting paradigms. In particular, the original idea of the World Englishes movement was to go beyond the monocentric (or, in turn, duocentric or oligocentric) model to a pluricentric one. However, rather than reducing the complexity of World Englishes to a multiplication of single varieties, the objective ought to be to move towards a conceptualization which sees them as reciprocally contaminated in a fluid and dynamic process. Hence, the World English ethos could be conceptualized as a living ecosystem in which different elements inevitably influence one another to different degrees, even if we accept the idea that they are separately identifiable in abstract terms.

In other words, although within a certain inflexible tradition English has been dichotomically divided between standard and non-standard varieties, the World Englishes ethos has represented an epistemic shift from a monolithic conception of English to a pluralized one. At the same time, a new change is demanded within the WE paradigm itself. Indeed, the conceptualization based on a plurality of single entities can be further developed into the idea of a multifaceted, flexible, and dynamic system.

The concept of World Englishes has been criticized for somehow neglecting the existence of a standard of languages, but it is exactly the need to move beyond models which are inherently artifices which allows the concept of WE to constantly revitalize itself. Thus, this paradigm ultimately offers a reflexive standpoint which transcends preconceived categories.

From this perspective, instead of trying to detect the culprits responsible for the changes that the English language is undergoing, with the aim of impeding such variations in the name of the preservation of the beauty of the language, it is more fruitful to investigate the sociolinguistic reasons behind this evolution and to acknowledge the potential inherent in linguistic diversity. Such heterogeneity is not to be intended as the diversification of the same pure original entity, or as the pluralization of a sole variety, but rather as the expression of a living language system or a language network, in which original input is acquired, transmitted, and put into circulation in a continuous process of cross-fertilization.

Consequently, if one of the metaphors used in the narrative about the English language is to describe it as a river, we could instead affirm that it is a complex water system in which rivers, torrents, and streams of different kinds constantly intersect, interact, and merge.

7.2 Creativity and innovation

Word-formation processes may be seen as a confirmation of "the general creative capability of the human mind to construct and label new concepts, also by combining existing mental categories" (Onysko/Michel 2010: 2). In particular, Booij stresses the idea of "rule-governed creativity" (2005: 6), as word formations tend to follow specific linguistic rules which, however, are not always obvious. When formations violate such rules, they appear inappropriate, although not necessarily impossible (see Bauer 1983: 293–295), and this process seems to confirm people's ability to mold and operate lexical resources.

Conclusions

The analysis of neologisms offers useful insights into the development of a language, or of a specific variety, not only from a purely linguistic perspective but also in socio-cultural terms, as lexical changes often represent the expression of social changes within a community of users. New formations in English often concern the IT sphere, but this work has shown that a vast range of semantic areas are involved. However, any contribution on lexical innovation is somehow deemed to struggle when attempting to keep pace with the ongoing changes which English varieties undergo.

The lexicon of varieties changes in line with socio-political realities, which contribute to developing creative and vibrant word stocks pertaining to the various domains of public life. Lexical items can be created within a specific linguistic context and then be adopted by others, to the extent that the original varietal labels may be lost, and such items are recognized as part of the English lexicon at large.

World Englishes are commonly considered creative from a lexical perspective. Scholars often talk about creativity in World Englishes as the tendency to go beyond the conventions of the L1. Although such transcendence needs to be problematized and can in turn be the expression of a wide range of situations, lexical creation can be described as being at the same time unconventional and remarkably operative. These creative processes fulfill a series of purposes such as that of an economical use of the language or the need to plug a lexical gap. In particular, World Englishes present several instances of interim and *ad hoc* word formations.[1] These expressions are not statistically frequent and represent nonce-formations which may be subsequently abandoned. However, their usage calls for deeper investigation as their speakers often exploit creative encoding possibilities, thereby confirming the inventive potential inherent in World Englishes.

The debate on whether a neologism used in a specific variety should be considered an English neological form from a wider perspective remains open. However, the constant contact between the different varieties usually allows for mutual intelligibility; thus, a varietal nonce-formation may develop into a neologism and may undergo the process of lexicalization, institutionalization, and hypostatization (see Section 3.3) in the variety in which it originated and may experience the same process synchronically or diachronically in other varieties. In this view, lexical innovation is not intended simply as the creation of new formations, but also as the sharing of words which, albeit commonly described as belonging to a specific variety, become part of a wider repertoire available to other users.

The inclusion of a word in a dictionary is only one of the elements which contribute to innovation from a lexical perspective, but when dealing with a language whose reach is global, such as English, it represents an important moment for the constant revitalization of a language. Of course, English dictionaries have always, to differing degrees, been receptive to words originating in non-British varieties, although unevenly and inconsistently. As Salazar (2014) notes, what makes this process highly significant is the continual growth of opportunities and challenges for the revitalization of English at large that World Englishes bring with them.

7.3 Final implications

The theoretical and empirical perspectives in this work are primarily of interest to World Englishes research but may also contribute to advancing our understanding about the role of English in the world from a broader socio-cultural viewpoint, as well as to informing critical debate across our academic and professional communities. This study shows the importance of investigating lexical developments when observing the evolution of WE and argues for the need to go beyond a purely structuralist framework and to include a broader discursive and sociological perspective in any lexical investigation.

The operative approach adopted in the analytical section of this work is, to a certain degree, territorial as that is functional to the detection of lexical dynamics which can corroborate or refute the theory of lexical contamination across varieties. However, the analysis itself contributes to demonstrating the aterritoriality of the World Englishes paradigm, determined by the unprecedented transnational linguistic contamination which English undergoes.

On a practical note, while not being purely a corpus-based study, this work also suggests implications for corpus linguistics by inferring that structural descriptions drawn from corpora may be insufficient to capture the complexity and dynamicity of different uses of English around the world. At the same time, the investigation of fluid and evolving forms of English may benefit from the use of corpora if they provide satisfactory contextual information. More specifically, this study has confirmed that corpora such as ICE and GloWbE can both provide revealing data, and their features can be fruitfully exploited if one needs high cross-comparability (ICE) or adequate size (GloWbE) to conduct lexical investigations. The combination of corpora with different structural characteristics should not be seen as a manipulative attempt to adopt tools designed for different purposes in order to reach a single aim, but rather as a potential way to go beyond feature-based descriptions and to learn more about language practice.

However, an urgent priority at this point is, as Nelson and Ozón rightly observe, "to develop a more flexible corpus design, and specifically one that allows for individual local differences while at the same time ensuring maximum comparability across corpora" (2018: 158). This should be done with the awareness that the collection of big quantities of data cannot be an end in itself, but a means by which to explore and explain byzantine language dynamics, especially when dealing with changeable and versatile (and to some extent mercurial and protean) language compounds such as World Englishes.

Consequently, corpora continue to represent a valuable resource, although the complexification of language varieties determines the need for higher sophistication in corpus analysis, and efforts should be made to include more relevant contextual and background knowledge and user information. This analysis also advocates that web-derived corpora represent a vital opportunity to study varieties on a large scale, provided that cautious analytical processing is conducted.

The use of lexicographic resources is remarkably beneficial for the investigation of WE from different perspectives: on the one hand, codification and subsequent legitimization attitudes towards a variety are enhanced by such resources; on the other hand, lexicography can enrich the debate on crucial issues such as the adequacy of variety labels and their exclusiveness (Ooi 2018).

In this respect, this study suggests that the attribution of a specific label to a variety often rests on fragile ground and cannot be based solely on a country's boundaries, given that linguistic borders do not always correspond to national ones. Moreover, lemmas that index a specific variety in mainstream dictionaries should be considered with caution, given their unstable contours, although they can also offer precious insights into the cross-fertilization potential of WE from a lexical perspective.

Ultimately, this work has shown that the investigation of World Englishes is not only interesting and fascinating, even from a merely descriptive standpoint, but is also crucial as it inherently implies the expansion of linguistic perspectives and the tackling of new challenges. Indeed, given the growing research interest in World Englishes that we are experiencing, one may feel that the field will soon be saturated. Instead, we have only just started to deepen our understanding of a series of regional and macroregional varieties and their potential for becoming new linguistic epicenters (Gries/Bernaisch 2016), as well as of the porousness of their boundaries and the volatility of some varietal labels. With this in mind, the researcher's interest should not be to focus exclusively on frequencies and distributions in order to corroborate preexisting theories on the overuse, or underuse, of certain expressions across varieties. Rather, a fruitful overarching aim is to try to explore innovative lexical forms through qualitative patterns of convergence and divergence, which may lead to a more nuanced appreciation of the linguistic ecology of World Englishes and the mutual stimuli produced by their lexical repertoires. In this vein, further steps in the field should aim to present a more refined problematization of the processes of lexical cross-fertilization, with the awareness that linguistic repertoires are geographically, culturally, and anthropologically hybrid.

Note

1 This holds true also for idiomatic and metaphorical expressions which, however, were not the focal point of this analysis.

Appendix 1
OED March 2016 Hong Kong English updates[1]

- *char siu*: chiefly Hong Kong English, Singapore English and Malaysian English) in Cantonese cookery: roast pork marinated in a sweet and savoury sauce, typically served sliced into thin strips.
- *compensated dating*: (in Japan and Hong Kong contexts) a form of paid escort work in which a young woman provides companionship or sexual favours to an older man in exchange for money or luxury items.
- *dai pai dong*: (Hong Kong English) a traditional licenced street stall, typically with a small seating area, selling cooked food at low prices.
- *kaifong*: (Hong Kong English) an association formed to promote and protect the interests of a neighbourhood.
- *guanxi*: in Chinese contexts: a network of personal connections and social relationships one can use for professional or other advantage.
- *lucky money*: money believed to bring good luck; *spec.* (in Chinese contexts) such money placed in a red envelope and given as a gift.
- *sandwich class*: (general and Hong Kong English) a class of people characterized as having moderate incomes; *esp.* (chiefly Hong Kong English) a class of people whose incomes exceed the limits for public housing but who cannot afford to purchase private homes.
- *milk tea*: any of various drinks made with tea and milk or cream; *esp.* a drink originating in Hong Kong, made with black tea and evaporated or condensed milk.
- *shroff*: (Hong Kong English) more fully *shroff office*: a cashier's office or payment booth, especially at a car park.
- *sitting-out area*: a place for sitting outdoors; *spec.* (chiefly Hong Kong English) a small public space with seating in a built-up urban area.
- *siu mei*: (Hong Kong English) in Cantonese cookery: marinated meat roasted on a spit over an open fire or in a wood-burning rotisserie oven.
- *yum cha*: in Chinese contexts: a meal eaten in the morning or early afternoon, typically consisting of dim sum and hot tea.
- *wet market*: (S.E. Asian English) a market for the sale of fresh meat, fish, and produce.

Note

1 "New Hong Kong English Words". See: https://public.oed.com/the-oed-today/recent-updates-to-the-oed/previous-updates/march-2016-update/new-hong-kong-english-words/ (accessed 05/12/2017).

Definitions are taken from the Oxford English Dictionary Online. See: www.oed.com (accessed 06/12/2017).

Appendix 2
OED June 2015 Updates from Tagalog and Filipino usage of English[1]

- *advanced*: of a clock or watch: indicating a time ahead of the correct time.
- *bahala na*: expressing an attitude of optimistic acceptance or fatalistic resignation, especially in acknowledging that the outcome of an uncertain or difficult situation is beyond one's control or is preordained; 'que sera sera'. Hence also as noun: an approach to life characterized by this attitude.
- *balikbayan*: a Filipino visiting or returning to the Philippines after a period of living in another country.
- *balikbayan box*: a carton shipped or brought to the Philippines from another country by a Filipino who has been living overseas, typically containing items such as food, clothing, toys, and household products.
- *baon*: money, food, or other provisions taken to school, work, or on a journey.
- *barangay*: in the Philippines: a village, suburb, or other demarcated neighborhood; a small territorial and administrative district forming the most local level of government.
- *barkada*: a group of friends.
- *barong*: short for *barong tagalog*.
- *barong tagalog*: a lightweight, embroidered shirt for men, worn untucked and traditionally made of piña or a similar vegetable fiber.
- *baro't saya*: a traditional Philippine costume for women, consisting of a collarless blouse and a long wrap-around skirt.
- *batchmate*: a member of the same graduation class as another; a classmate. Also in extended use.
- *buko*: the gelatinous flesh of an unripe (green-husked) coconut.
- *buko juice*: a drink made from the clear watery liquid inside unripe coconuts; coconut water.
- *buko water*: buko juice.
- *carnap*: to steal (a motor vehicle).

Appendix 2   137

- *carnapper*: a person who steals a motor vehicle; a car thief.
- *comfort room*: a room in a public building or workplace furnished with amenities such as facilities for resting, personal hygiene, and storage of personal items (now rare); (later) a public toilet (now chiefly Philippine English).
- *despedida*: more fully *despedida party*; a social event honoring someone who is about to depart on a journey or leave an organization; a going-away party.
- *dirty kitchen*: a kitchen where everyday cooking is done by household staff, as distinct from a kitchen that is purely for show or for special use by the owner of the house.
- *estafa*: criminal deception, fraud; dishonest dealing.
- *gimmick*: a night out with friends.
- *go down*: to get off a vehicle.
- *halo-halo*: A dessert made of mixed fruits, sweet beans, milk, and shaved ice, typically topped with purple yam, crème caramel, and ice cream.
- *high blood*: angry, agitated.
- *kikay*: a flirtatious girl or woman. Also: a girl or woman interested in beauty products and fashion.
- *kikay kit*: a soft case in which a woman's toiletries and cosmetics are stored.
- *KKB*: '*kaniya-kaniyang bayad*', literally 'each one pays their own', used especially to indicate that the cost of a meal is to be shared. Also as adjective.
- *kuya*: an elder brother. Also used as a respectful title or form of address for an older man.
- *Mabuhay*: an exclamation of salutation or greeting: long live! good luck (to you)! hurrah! cheers!
- *mani-pedi*: a beauty treatment comprising both a manicure and a pedicure.
- *pan de sal*: a yeast-raised bread roll made of flour, eggs, sugar and salt, widely consumed in the Philippines, especially for breakfast.
- *pasalubong*: a gift or souvenir given to a friend or relative by a person who has returned from a trip or arrived for a visit.
- *presidentiable*: a person who is a likely or confirmed candidate for president.
- *pulutan*: food or snacks provided as an accompaniment to alcoholic drinks.
- *salvage*: to apprehend and execute (a suspected criminal) without trial.
- *sari-sari store*: a small neighborhood store selling a variety of goods.
- *sinigang*: in Filipino cookery: a type of soup made with meat, shrimp, or fish and flavored with a sour ingredient such as tamarind or guava.

Appendix 2

- *suki*: a buyer or seller involved in an arrangement whereby a customer regularly purchases products or services from the same provider in exchange for favorable treatment. Also: the arrangement itself.
- *utang na loob*: a sense of obligation to return a favor owed to someone.

Note

1 "New Filipino Words List". See: https://public.oed.com/the-oed-today/recent-updates-to-the-oed/previous-updates/june-2015-update/new-filipino-words-list/ (accessed 05/12/2017).

    All definitions are taken from the Oxford English Dictionary Online. See www.oed.com (accessed 05/12/2017).

References

Abdulaziz, Mohamed 1991. East Africa. In Cheshire, Jenny (ed.) *English around the World: Sociolinguistic Perspectives*. Cambridge: Cambridge University Press. 391–401.

Adedimeji, Mahfouz A. 2007. The Linguistic Features of Nigerian English and their Implications for 21st Century English Pedagogy. *Abuja Communicator* 3/1. 57–174.

Adegbija, Efurosibina 1989. Lexico-semantic Variation in Nigerian English. *World Englishes* 8/2. 165–177.

Adegbija, Efurosibina 2004. The Domestication of English in Nigeria. In Awonusi, Segun / Babalola, Emmanuel A. (eds) *The Domestication of English in Nigeria: A Festschrift in Honour of Abiodun Adetugbo*. Lagos, Nigeria: University of Lagos Press. 20–44.

Adeyanju, Dele 2009. Idiomatic Variation in Nigerian English: Implications for Standardization in the Context of Globalization. *Journal of English Studies* 7. 7–22.

Aitchison, Jean 2005. Language Change. In Cobley, Paul (ed.) *The Routledge Companion to Semiotics and Linguistics*. London: Routledge. 95–104.

Ajani, Timothy T. 2007. Is there Indeed a 'Nigerian English'? *Journal of Humanities & Social Sciences* 1/1.

Akindele, Femi / Adegbite, Wale 1992. *The Sociology and Politics of English Language in Nigeria*. Ile-Ife, Nigeria: Debiyi-Iwa.

Akmajian, Adrian / Demers, Richard A. / Farmer, Ann K. / Harnish, Robert M. (eds) 2010. *Linguistics: An Introduction to Language and Communication*. 6th ed. Cambridge, MA: MIT Press.

Alabi, Victoria A. 2000. Semantics of Occupational Lexis in Nigerian English. *World Englishes* 19/1. 107–112.

Algeo, John 1977. Blends, a Structural and Systemic View. *American Speech* 52. 47–64.

Algeo, John 1980. Where Do All the New Words Come From? *American Speech* 55. 264–277.

Allsopp, Richard 1996. *The Dictionary of Caribbean English Usage*. Oxford: Oxford University Press.

References

Allsopp, Richard 2010. *New Register of Caribbean English Usage*. Jamaica: University of the West Indies Press.

Alo, Moses A. 2004. Context and Language Variation: The EL2 Example. In Oyeleye, Lekan (ed.) *Language and Discourse in Society*. Ibadan: Hope Publication. 73–82.

Alo, Moses A. / Mesthrie, Rajend 2004. Nigerian English: Morphology and Syntax. In Kortmann, Bernd / Schneider, Edgar W. / Burridge, Kate / Mesthrie, Rajend / Upton, Clive (eds) *A Handbook of Varieties of English*, vol. 2. Berlin: Mouton de Gruyter. 813–827.

Ansaldo, Umberto 2004. The Evolution of Singapore English: Finding the Matrix. In Lim, Lisa (ed.) *Singapore English: A Grammatical Description*. Amsterdam/Philadelphia: John Benjamins. 127–149.

Aronoff, Mark 1983. Potential Words, Actual Words, Productivity and Frequency. *Proceedings of the 13th International Congress of Linguists, Tokyo*. 163–171.

Aronoff, Mark / Anshen, Frank 1998. Morphology and the Lexicon: Lexicalization and Productivity. In Spencer, Andrew / Zwicky, Arnold M. (eds) *The Handbook of Morphology*. Cambridge, MA: Blackwell. 237–247.

Avis, Walter S. l967. *A Dictionary of Canadianisms on Historical Principles*. Toronto: Gage.

Ayto, John 2004. Newspapers and Neologisms. In Aitchison, Jean / Lewis, Diana M. (eds) *New Media Language*. London: Routledge. 182–186.

Baayen, R. Harald / Lieber, Rochelle 1991. Productivity and English Derivation: A Corpus-Based Study. *Linguistics* 29. 801–843.

Balteiro, Isabel 2007. *A Contribution to the Study of Conversion in English*. Münster: Waxmann.

Bamgbose, Ayo 1982. Standard Nigerian English: Issues of Identification. In Kachru, Braj B. (ed.) *The Other Tongue: English across Cultures*. Urbana, IL: University of Illinois Press. 99–111.

Bamiro, Edmund 1994. Lexico-semantic Variation in Nigerian English. *World Englishes* 13/1. 47–60.

Banjo, Ayo / Young, Peter 1982. On Editing a Second-Language Dictionary: The Proposed Dictionary of West African English (DWAE). *English World-Wide* 3. 87–91.

Bao, Zhiming 2005. The Aspectual System of Singapore English and the Systemic Substratist Explanation. *Linguistics* 41. 237–267.

Bao, Zhiming 2018. World Englishes and Contact Varieties: Clustering in a Substrate Influence. In Low, Ee Ling / Pakir, Anne (eds) *World Englishes: Rethinking Paradigms*. Abingdon: Routledge. 132–148.

Bao, Zhiming / Hong, Huaqing 2006. Diglossia and Register Variation in Singapore English. *World Englishes* 25/1. 105–114.

Barber, Katherine 1999. *The Canadian Oxford Dictionary*. Oxford: Oxford University Press.

Barnhart, David K. 2007. A Calculus for New Words. *Dictionaries* 28. 132–138.

Bauer, Laurie 1983. *English Word-Formation*. Cambridge: Cambridge University Press.

Bauer, Laurie 2001. *Morphological Productivity*. Cambridge: Cambridge University Press.

References

Bauer, Laurie 2005. Productivity: Theories. In Štekauer, Pavol / Lieber, Rochelle (eds) *Handbook of Word-Formation*. Dordrecht: Springer. 315–334.
Bauer, Laurie 2006. Compounds and Minor Word-Formation Types. In Aarts, Bas / McMahon, April (eds) *The Handbook of English Linguistics*. Oxford: Blackwell. 483–506.
Bauer, Laurie / Huddleston, Rodney 2002. Lexical Word-Formation. In Huddleston, Rodney / Pullum, Geoffrey (eds) *The Cambridge Grammar of the English Language*. Cambridge: Cambridge University Press. 1621–1721.
Baumgardner, Robert J. 1998. Word-Formation in Pakistani English. *English World-Wide* 19. 205–246.
Bautista, Maria Lourdes S. 1997. The Lexicon of Philippine English. In Bautista, Maria Lourdes S. (ed.) *English Is an Asian Language: The Philippine Context*. Manila: Macquarie Library. 49–72.
Bautista, Maria Lourdes S. / Butler, Susan 2000. *Anvil-Macquarie Dictionary of Philippine English for High School*. Pasig City: Anvil.
Beal, Joan 2009. Three Hundred Years of Prescriptivism (and Counting). In Tieken-Boon van Ostade, Ingrid / van der Wurff, Wim (eds) *Current Issues in Late Modern English*. Bern: Peter Lang. 35–56.
Bekker, Ian 2012. South African English as a Late 19th-Century Extraterritorial Variety. *English World-Wide* 33/2. 127–146.
Biermeier, Thomas 2008. *Word Formation in New Englishes: A Corpus-Based Analysis*. Berlin: LIT.
Biermeier, Thomas 2017. Lexical Trends in Philippine English Revisited. *Philippine ESL Journal* 19. 25–44.
Blench, Roger 2013. *A Dictionary of Belizean English*. Available at: www.rogerblench.info/Language/English/Belizean%20English%20dictionary.pdf (accessed 25/01/2018).
Bloomfield, Leonard 1933. *Language*. New York: Holt, Rinehart and Winston.
Bokamba, Eyamba 1991. West Africa. In Cheshire, Jenny (ed.) *English around the World*. Cambridge: Cambridge University Press. 493–508.
Bokamba, Eyamba 1992. The Africanisation of English. In Kachru, Braj B. (ed.) *The Other Tongue: English across Cultures*. 2nd ed. Urbana: Illinois University Press. 125–174.
Bolton, Kingsley 2005. Where WE Stands: Approaches, Issues, and Debates in World Englishes. *World Englishes* 24/1. 69–83.
Bolton, Kingsley 2013. World Englishes, Globalisation, and Language Worlds. In Johannesson, Nils-Lennart / Melchers, Gunnel / Björkman, Beyza (eds) *Of Butterflies and Birds, of Dialects and Genres: Essays in Honour of Philip Shaw*. Stockholm: Acta Universitatis Stockholmiensis. 227–251.
Bolton, Kingsley / Butler, Susan 2004. Dictionaries and the Stratification of Vocabulary: Towards a New Lexicography for Philippine English. *World Englishes* 23/1. 91–112.
Bolton, Kingsley / Graddol, David 2012. English in China Today. *English Today* 28/3. 3–9.
Bonfiglio, Thomas P. 2007. Language, Racism and Ethnicity. In Hellinger, Marlis / Pauwels, Ann (eds) *Handbook of Language and Communication: Diversity and Change*. Berlin: de Gruyter. 619–650.

Booij, Geert 2005. *The Grammar of Words: An Introduction to Linguistic Morphology*. Oxford: Oxford University Press.

Borlongan, Ariane Macalinga 2016. Relocating Philippine English in Schneider's Dynamic Model. *Asian Englishes* 18/3. 1–10.

Bowerman, Sean 2004. White South Africa English: Phonology. In Kortmann, Bernd / Burridge, Kate / Mesthrie, Rajend / Schneider, Edgar W. / Upton, Clive (eds) *A Handbook of Varieties of English*, vol. 1: *Phonology*. Berlin: Mouton de Gruyter. 164–167.

Branford, William (ed.) 1987. *The South African Pocket Dictionary*. Cape Town: Oxford University Press.

Brinton, Laurel J. / Traugott, Elizabeth C. 2005. *Lexicalization and Language Change*. Cambridge: Cambridge University Press.

Bruthiaux, Paul 2003. Squaring the Circles: Issues in Modeling English Worldwide. *International Journal of Applied Linguistics* 13/2. 159–178.

Brutt-Griffler, Janina / Samimy, Keiko 2001. Transcending the Nativeness Paradigm. *World Englishes* 20/1. 99–106.

Buang, Sri Norazrin / Halim, Nurulhuda Abdul / Ramakresinin, Shamala 2008. Malay Lexical Borrowings in Singapore Colloquial English. In Hashim, Azirah (ed.) *Journal of Modern Languages* 18. 143–162.

Budohoska, Natalia 2014. *English in Kenya or Kenyan English?* Frankfurt am Main: Peter Lang.

Buregeya, Alfred 2006. Grammatical Features of Kenyan English and their Extent of Acceptability. *English World-Wide* 27. 199–216.

Buschfeld, Sarah / Kautzsch, Alexander 2017. Towards an Integrated Approach to Postcolonial and Non-Postcolonial Englishes. *World Englishes* 36/1. 104–126.

Cabré, M. Teresa 1999. *Terminology: Theory, Methods and Application*. Amsterdam. John Benjamins.

Cassidy, Frederic G. 1985. *Dictionary of American Regional English*. Cambridge, MA: Harvard University Press.

Cassidy, Frederic G. / Le Page, Robert 1967. *Dictionary of Jamaican English*. Cambridge: Cambridge University Press.

Cassidy, Frederic G. / Le Page, Robert 2002. *Dictionary of Jamaican English*. 2nd ed. Kingston: University of West Indies Press.

Choi, Jungwha 2006. Interpreting Neologisms Used in Korea's Rapidly Changing Society: Delivering the Meaning of Neologisms in Simultaneous Interpretation. *Meta: journal des traducteurs / Meta: Translators' Journal* 51/2. 188–201.

Clark, Herbert H. 1996. *Using Language*. Cambridge: Cambridge University Press.

Clyne, Michael G. 1991. *Community Languages: The Australian Experience*. Cambridge: Cambridge University Press.

Connor Martin, Katherine 2014. Is it 'Defriend' or 'Unfriend'? Available at: http://oupacademic.tumblr.com/post/75764162479/unfriend-defriend-usage-facebook (accessed 25/02/2018).

Cook, Paul 2010. *Exploiting Linguistic Knowledge to Infer Properties of Neologisms*. PhD thesis. University of Toronto. Available at: www.cs.toronto.edu/~pcook/Cook2010.pdf (accessed 25/03/2017).

Cook, Paul / Brinton, Laurel J. 2017. Building and Evaluating Web Corpora Representing National Varieties of English. *Language Resources and Evaluation* 51. 643–662.
Coupland, Nik / Jaworski, Adam (eds) 2004. *Metalanguage*. New York: de Gruyter.
Croft, William A. 2000. *Explaining Language Change*. Harlow: Longman Linguistic Library.
Crystal, David 1997. *A Dictionary of Linguistics and Phonetics*. 4th ed. Oxford: Blackwell.
Crystal, David 2000. Investigating Nonceness: Lexical Innovation and Lexicographic Coverage. In Boenig, Robert / Davis, Kathleen (eds) *Manuscript, Narrative, Lexicon: Essays on Literary and Cultural Transmission in Honor of Whitney F. Bolton*. Lewisburg: Bucknell University Press. 218–231.
Crystal, David 2003. *The Cambridge Encyclopedia of the English Language*. 2nd ed. Cambridge: Cambridge University Press.
Crystal, David 2006. *Words, Words, Words*. Oxford: Oxford University Press.
Crystal, David 2011. *The Story of English in 100 Words*. London: Profile Books.
Cummings, Patrick / Wolf, Hans-Georg 2011. *A Dictionary of Hong Kong English: Words from the Fragrant Harbour*. Hong Kong: Hong Kong University Press.
Curzan, Anne 2000. The Compass of the Vocabulary. In Mugglestone, Lynda (ed.) *Lexicography and the OED: Pioneers in the Untrodden Forest*. Oxford: Oxford University Press.
Dasgupta, Probal 1993. *The Otherness of English: India's Auntie Tongue Syndrome*. New Delhi: SAGE.
Davies, Alan 2003. *The Native Speaker: Myth and Reality*. Clevedon: Multilingual Matters.
Davies, Mark / Fuchs, Robert 2015. Expanding Horizons in the Study of World Englishes with the 1.9 Billion Word Global Web-based English Corpus (GloWbE). *English World-Wide* 36/1. 1–28.
Davis, Matthew H. / Di Betta, Anna Maria / Macdonald, Mark J. E. / Gaskell, Gareth 2009. Learning and Consolidation of Novel Spoken Words. *Journal of Cognitive Neuroscience* 21/4. 802–820.
de Saussure, Ferdinand 1959. *Course in General Linguistics*. New York: Philosophical Library.
de Swaan, Abram 2013/2002. *Words of the World: The Global Language System*. Cambridge: Polity Press.
de Vaan, Laura / Schreuder, Rob / Baayen, Harald 2007. Neologisms and Lexical Memory: Regular Morphologically Complex Neologisms Leave Detectable Traces in the Mental Lexicon. *Mental Lexicon* 2/1. 1–23.
DeCamp, David 1971. Toward a Generative Analysis of a Post-creole Speech Continuum. In Hymes, Dell (ed.) *Pidginization and Creolization of Languages*. Cambridge: Cambridge University Press. 349–370.
Delbridge, Arthur, et al. (eds) 1981. *The Macquarie Dictionary*. Sydney: Macquarie Library.
Deterding, David 2007. *Dialects of English: Singapore English*. Edinburgh: Edinburgh University Press.

Dictionary Unit for South African English (ed.) 2002. *South African Concise Oxford Dictionary*. Cape Town: Oxford University Press Southern Africa.

Dolezal, Frederic 2006. World Englishes and Lexicography. In Kachru, Braj B. / Kachru, Yamuna / Nelson, Cecil L. (eds) *The Handbook of World Englishes*. Malden, MA: Blackwell. 694–708.

Edwards, Alison / Laporte, Samantha 2015. Outer and Expanding Circle Englishes: The Competing Roles of Norm Orientation and Proficiency Levels. *English World-Wide* 36/2. 135–169.

Elmes, Simon 2001. *The Routes of English*. London: BBC Adult Learning.

Epstein, Mikhail 2012. *The Transformative Humanities: A Manifesto*. New York: Bloomsbury.

Esteves, Vanessa Reis / Hurst, Nicolas 2009. Varieties of English: South African English. *APPI Journal* 9/2. 1–10.

European Commission 2011. *Lingua Franca: Chimera or Reality?* Available at: http://cordis.europa.eu/fp7/ict/language-technologies/docs/lingua-franca-en.pdf (accessed 25/02/2018).

Evans, Stephen 2011. Hong Kong English: The Growing Pains of a New Variety. *Asian Englishes* 14. 22–45.

Evans, Stephen 2015. Word-Formation in Hong Kong English: Diachronic and Synchronic Perspectives. *Asian Englishes* 17/2. 116–131.

Fairclough, Marta 2003. El (denominado) Spanglish en Estados Unidos: Polémicas y realidades. *Revista Internacional de Lingüística Iberoamericana* 2. 185–204.

Fandrych, Ingrid 2004. *Non-Morphematic Word-Formation Processes: A Multi-Level Approach to Acronyms, Blends, Clippings and Onomatopoeia*. Unpublished PhD thesis, University of the Free State, Bloemfontein.

Fardon, Richard / Furniss, Graham 1994. *African Languages, Development and the State*. London: Routledge.

Farquharson, Joseph / Jones, Byron 2014. In Coleman, Julie (ed.) *Global English Slang: Methodologies and Perspectives*. London: Routledge. 116–125.

Ferguson, Charles 1959. Diglossia. *Word* 15. 325–340.

Ferguson, Charles 1983. Language Planning and Language Change. In Cobarrubias, Juan / Fishman, Joshua (eds) *Progress in Language Planning: International Perspectives*. Berlin: Mouton. 29–40.

Ferguson, Charles 1991. Diglossia Revisited. *Southwest Journal of Linguistics* 10/1. 214–234.

Fernández-Domínguez, Jesús 2010. Productivity vs. Lexicalization: Frequency-Based Hypotheses on Word-Formation. *Poznań Studies in Contemporary Linguistics* 46/2. 193–219.

Fischer, Roswitha. 1998. *Lexical Change in Present-Day English: A Corpus-Based Study of the Motivation, Institutionalization, and Productivity of Creative Neologisms*. Tübingen: Gunter Narr.

Fong, Vivienne / Wee, Lionel 2002. 'Singlish': Used and Abused. *Asian Englishes* 5/1. 18–39.

Gaskell, Gareth / Dumay, Nicolas. 2003. Lexical Competition and the Acquisition of Novel Words. *Cognition* 89. 105–132.

Görlach, Manfred 1995. *More Englishes: New Studies in Varieties of English 1988–1994.* Amsterdam: John Benjamins.
Graddol, David 1997. *The Future of English? A Guide to Forecasting the Popularity of the English Language in the 21st Century.* London: British Council.
Graddol, David 2006. *English Next.* London: British Council.
Graddol, David 2010. *English Next: India.* London: British Council.
Graddol, David / Leith, Dick / Swann, Joan 1996. *English: History, Diversity and Change.* London: Routledge.
Greenbaum, Sidney (ed.) 1996. *Comparing English Worldwide: The International Corpus of English.* Oxford: Clarendon Press.
Gries, Stefan T. / Bernaisch, Tobias J. 2016. Exploring Epicenters Empirically: Focus on South Asian Englishes. *English World-Wide* 37/1. 1–25.
Hackert, Stephanie 2012. *The Emergence of the English Native Speaker: A Chapter in Nineteenth-Century Linguistic Thought.* Berlin, Boston: de Gruyter.
Haugen, Einar 1950. The Analysis of Linguistic Borrowing. *Language* 26. 210–231.
Hickey, Raymond 2004. Glossary of Terms. In Hickey, Raymond (ed.) *Legacies of Colonial English: Studies in Transported Dialects.* Cambridge: Cambridge University Press.
Hickey, Raymond 2012. Standard English and Standards of English. In Hickey, Raymond (ed.) *Standards of English: Codified Varieties around the World.* Cambridge: Cambridge University Press. 1–33.
Hickey, Raymond 2014. *A Dictionary of Varieties of English.* Chichester: Wiley Blackwell.
Hohenhaus, Peter 2007. How to Do (Even More) Things with Nonce Words (Other than Naming). In Munat, Judith (ed.) *Lexical Creativity, Texts and Contexts.* Amsterdam: Benjamins. 15–38.
Holm, John / Shilling, Alison W. 1982. *Dictionary of Bahamian English.* Cold Spring, NY: Lexik House.
Holmes, David 1991. Vocabulary Richness and the Prophetic Voice. *Literary and Linguistic Computing* 6/4. 259–268.
Holmes, Janet 2008. National Languages and Language Planning. In *An Introduction to Sociolinguistics.* 3rd ed. London: Pearson Longman. 98–124.
Honey, John 1997. *Language is Power: The Story of Standard English and its Enemies.* London: Faber and Faber.
House, Juliane 1999. Misunderstanding in Intercultural Communication: Interactions in English as a Lingua Franca and the Myth of Mutual Intelligibility. In Gnutzmann, Claus (ed.) *Teaching and Learning English as a Global Language.* Tübingen: Stauffenburg. 73–89.
Hundt, Marianne / Nesselhauf, Nadja / Biewer, Carolin (eds) 2007. *Corpus Linguistics and the Web.* Amsterdam: Rodopi.
Isingoma, Bebwa 2014. Lexical and Grammatical Features of Ugandan English. *English Today* 30/2. 51–56.
Jenkins, Jennifer 2003. *World Englishes: A Resource Book for Students.* London: Routledge.

Jibril, Munzali 1982. Nigerian English: An Introduction. In Pride, John B. (ed.) *New Englishes*. Rowley, MA: Newbury House. 73–84.

John, Binoo K. 2007. *Entry from Backside Only: Hazaar Fundas of Indian English*. New Delhi: Penguin Books.

Jowitt, David 1991. *Nigerian English Usage: An Introduction*. Ikeja: Longman Nigeria.

Kaan, Aondover Theophilus / Amase, Emmanuel Lanior / Tsavmbu, Alexis Aondover 2013. Nigerian English: Identifying Semantic Features as Variety Markers. *IOSR Journal of Humanities and Social Science (IOSR-JHSS)* 16/5. 76–80.

Kachru, Braj B. 1981. The Pragmatics of Non-native Varieties of English. In Smith, Larry (ed.) *English for Cross-cultural Communication*. London: Palgrave. 15–39.

Kachru, Braj B. 1983. *The Indianization of English*. New Delhi: Oxford University Press.

Kachru, Braj B. 1985. Standards, Codification and Sociolinguistic Realism: The English Language in the Outer Circle. In Quirk, Randolph / Widdowson, Henry (eds) *English in the World: Teaching and Learning the Language and Literatures*. Cambridge: Cambridge University Press. 11–30.

Kachru, Braj B. 1992. Teaching World Englishes. In Kachru, Braj B. (ed.) *The Other Tongue: English across Cultures*. Urbana, IL: University of Illinois Press. 355–365.

Kachru, Braj B. 1997. World Englishes 2000: Resources for Research and Teaching. In Smith, Larry / Forman, Michael (eds) *World Englishes: Selected Essays*, vol. 14. Honolulu: University of Hawaii East-West Center. 209–251.

Kachru, Braj B. 2005. *Asian Englishes: Beyond the Canon*. Hong Kong: Hong Kong University Press.

Ke, I-Chung 2015. A Global Language, without a Global Culture: From Basic English to Global English. *English as a Global Language Education Journal* 1/1. 65–87.

Kerremans, Daphné 2015. *A Web of New Words: A Corpus-Based Study of the Conventionalization Process of English Neologisms*. Frankfurt am Main: Peter Lang.

Kortmann, Bernd / Burridge, Kate / Mesthrie, Rajend / Schneider, Edgar W. / Upton, Clive (eds) 2004. *A Handbook of Varieties of English*. Berlin: Mouton de Gruyter.

Kperogi, Farooq A. 2015. *Glocal English: The Changing Face and Forms of Nigerian English in a Global World*. New York: Peter Lang.

Krishnaswamy, N. / Burde, Archana 1998. *The Politics of Indian English: Linguistic Colonialisms and the Expanding English Empire*. Delhi: Oxford University Press.

Labov, William 2006. *The Social Stratification of English in New York City*. 2nd ed. Cambridge: Cambridge University Press.

Lambert, James 2018. Anglo-Indian Slang in Dictionaries on Historical Principles. *World Englishes* 1–13.

Lehrer, Adrienne 2003. Understanding Trendy Neologisms. *Italian Journal of Linguistics* 15/2. 369–322.

Lehrer, Adrienne 2007. Blendalicious. In Munat, Judith (ed.) *Lexical Creativity, Texts and Contexts*. Amsterdam: John Benjamins. 115–133.

Leimgruber, Jakob R. E. 2011. Singapore English. *Language and Linguistics Compass* 5/1. 47–62.
Leitner, Gerard 1992. English as Plurucentric Language. In Clyde, Michael (ed.) *Pluricentic Languages: Differing Norms in Different Nations*. Berlin: Mouton de Gruyter. 179–237.
Levchenko, Yaroslav 2010. *Neologism in the Lexical System of Modern English: On the Mass Media Material*. Munich: Grin.
Lim, Lisa / Foley, J.A. 2004. English in Singapore and Singapore English: Background and Methodology. In Lim, Lisa (ed.) *Singapore English: A Grammatical Description*. Philadelphia: John Benjamins. 1–18.
Lipka, Leonhard 2005. Lexicalisation and Institutionalisation: Revisited and Extended. *SKASE Journal of Theoretical Linguistics* 2. 40–42.
Lipka, Leonhard / Handl, Susanne / Falkner, Wolfgang 2004. Lexicalization and Institutionalization: The State of the Art in 2004. *SKASE Journal of Theoretical Linguistics* 1. 2–19.
Lippi-Green, Rosina 2011/1997. *English with an Accent: Language, Ideology, and Discrimination in the United States*. London: Routledge.
Loureiro-Porto, Lucía 2017. ICE vs GloWbE: Big Data and Corpus Compilation. *World Englishes* 36/3. 448–470.
Low, Ee Ling / Brown, Adam 2005. *English in Singapore: An Introduction*. Singapore: McGraw-Hill Education.
Lyons, John 1977. *Semantics*. Cambridge: Cambridge University Press.
Macalister, John 2007. Weka or Wooden? Nativization through Lexical Choice in New Zealand English. *World Englishes* 26/4. 492–506.
Mahboob, Ahmar / Liang, Jiawei 2014. Researching and Critiquing World Englishes. *Asian Englishes* 16/2. 125–140.
Mair, Christian 2011. Corpora and the New Englishes: Using the 'Corpus of Cyber-Jamaican' (CCJ) to Explore Research Perspectives for the Future. In Meunier, Fanny / de Cock, Sylvie / Gilquin, Gaëtanelle / Paquot, Magalie (eds) *A Taste for Corpora: In Honour of Sylviane Granger*. Amsterdam: John Benjamins. 209–236.
Mair, Christian 2013. The World System of Englishes: Accounting for the Transnational Importance of Mobile and Mediated Vernaculars. *English World-Wide* 34/3. 253–278.
Mair, Christian 2014. The Variability of Current World Englishes. In Green, Eugene / Meyer, Charles F. (eds) *Globalisation and the Transnational Impact of Non-standard Varieties*. Berlin, Boston: de Gruyter. 65–98.
Mair, Christian 2015. Response to Davies and Fuchs. *English World-Wide* 36/1. 29–33.
Makalela, Leketi 2007. Nativization of English among Bantu Language Speakers in South Africa. *Issues in Applied Linguistics* 15. 129–147.
Makoni, Sinfree / Pennycook, Alastair 2006. Disinventing and Reconstituting Languages. In Makoni, Sinfree / Pennycook, Alastair (eds) *Disinventing and Reconstituting Languages*. Clevedon: Multilingual Matters. 1–41.
Manning, Christopher D. / Schütze, Hinrich. 1999. *Foundations of Statistical Natural Language Processing*. Cambridge: MIT Press.

References

Mauranen, Anna 2003. The Corpus of English as Lingua Franca in Academic Settings. *TESOL Quarterly* 37. 513–527.

Mauranen, Anna 2012. *Exploring ELF: Academic English Shaped by Non-native Speakers*. Cambridge: Cambridge University Press.

McArthur, Tom (ed.) 1992. *The Oxford Companion to the English Language*. Oxford: Oxford University Press.

McArthur, Tom 1994. Organized Babel: English as a Global Lingua Franca. In Alatis, James E. (ed.) *Georgetown University Round Table on Languages and Linguistics 1994*. Washington, DC: Georgetown University Press. 233–242.

McArthur, Tom 1999. English in the World, in Africa, and in South Africa. *English Today* 15/1. 11–16.

McArthur, Tom 2002. *The Oxford Guide to World English*. Oxford: Oxford University Press.

McArthur, Tom 2003. World English, Euro English, Nordic English? *English Today* 19/1. 54–58.

McEnery, Tony / Ostler, Nick 2000. A New Agenda for Corpus Linguistics: Working with All of the World's Languages. *Literary and Linguistic Computing* 15/4. 403–420.

McKay, Sandra 2002. *Teaching English as an International Language*. Oxford: Oxford University Press.

Mehrotra, Raja Ram 1998. *Indian English*. Amsterdam: John Benjamins.

Meierkord, Christiane / Isingoma, Bebwa / Namyalo, Saudah 2016. (eds) *Ugandan English: Its Sociolinguistics, Structure and Uses in a Globalising Post-protectorate*. Amsterdam: John Benjamins.

Mesthrie, Rajend 2006. World Englishes and the Multilingual History of English. *World Englishes* 25/3–4. 381–390.

Metcalf, Allan 2002. *Predicting New Words*. Boston: Houghton Mifflin.

Miller, George A. 1995. WordNet: A Lexical Database for English. *Communications of the ACM*. 38/11. 39–41

Milroy, James 1992. *Linguistic Variation and Change*. Oxford: Oxford University Press.

Milroy, Jim 2002. The Legitimate Language: Giving a History to English. In Watts, Richard / Trudgill, Peter (eds) *Alternative Histories of English*. London: Routledge. 7–25.

Milroy, James / Milroy, Lesley 2012. *Authority in Language: Investigating Standard English*. 4th ed. Abingdon: Routledge.

Minkova, Donka / Stockwell, Robert 2006. English Words. In Aarts, Bas / McMahon, April (eds) *The Handbook of English Linguistics*. Oxford: Blackwell. 461–482.

Mitchell, Melanie 2009. *Complexity: A Guided Tour*. Oxford: Oxford University Press.

Modiano, Marko 1999. International English in the Global Village. *English Today* 15/2. 22–28.

Mollin, Sandra 2006. English as a Lingua Franca: A New Variety in the New Expanding Circle? *Nordic Journal of English Studies* 5/2. 41–57.

Momma, Haruko / Matto, Michael 2008. *A Companion to the History of the English Language*. Oxford: Blackwell.

Moore, Bruce 2016. *The Australian National Dictionary*. 2nd ed. Melbourne: Oxford University Press.

Mugglestone, Lynda 2007/1995. *Talking Proper: The Rise of Accent as Social Symbol*. 3rd ed. Oxford: Clarendon Press.

Munro, Murray J. / Derwing, Tracey M. 1995. Processing Time, Accent, and Comprehensibility in the Perception of Native and Foreign-Accented Speech. *Language and Speech* 38/3. 289–306.

Murray, James 1884. *Oxford English Dictionary*. Oxford: Clarendon Press.

Muysken, Pieter 2000. *Bilingual Speech: A Typology of Code-Mixing*. Cambridge: Cambridge University Press.

Nelson, Gerald / Ozón, Gabriel 2018. World Englishes and Corpus Linguistics. In Low, Ee Ling / Pakir, Anne (eds) *World Englishes: Rethinking Paradigms*. Abingdon: Routledge. 149–164.

Newmark, Peter 1988. *A Textbook of Translation*. New York: Prentice Hall.

O'Donovan, Ruth / O'Neil, Mary 2008. A Systematic Approach to the Selection of Neologisms for Inclusion in a Large Monolingual Dictionary. In *Proceedings of the 13th Euralex International Congress, Barcelona*. 571–579.

Odumuh, Adama 1993. *Sociolinguistics and Nigerian English*. Ibadan: Sam Bookman.

Ogilvie, Sarah 2012. *Words of the World: A Global History of the* Oxford English Dictionary. Cambridge: Cambridge University Press.

Onysko, Alexander 2016. Modeling World Englishes from the Perspective of Language Contact. *World Englishes* 35/2. 196–220.

Onysko, Alexander / Michel, Sascha 2010. Introduction: Unravelling the Cognitive in Word Formation. In Onysko, Alexander / Michel, Sascha (eds) *Cognitive Perspectives on Word Formation*. Berlin: de Gruyter. 1–25.

Ooi, Vincent 2018. Lexicography and World Englishes. In Low, Ee Ling / Pakir, Anne (eds) *World Englishes: Rethinking Paradigms*. Abingdon: Routledge. 165–182.

Owolabi, Dare 2012. Potential Words in English: Examples from Morphological Processes in Nigerian English. *English Today* 28/2. 47–50.

Pakir, Anne 1999. Bilingual Education with English as an Official Language: Sociocultural Implications. In Alatis, James E. / Tan, Ai-Hui (eds) *Georgetown University Round Table on Languages and Linguistics*. Washington, DC: Georgetown University Press. 341–349.

Patrick, Peter 2004. Jamaican Creole Morphology and Syntax. In Kortmann, Bernd / Schneider, Edgar / Upton, Clive / Mesthrie, Rajend / Burridge, Kate (eds) *A Handbook of Varieties of English*, vol. 2: *Morphology and Syntax*. Berlin, New York: Mouton de Gruyter. 407–438.

Pefianco Martin, Isabel 2014. Philippine English Revisited. *World Englishes* 33/1. 50–59.

Peprník, Jaroslav 2006. *English Lexicology*. Olomouc: Univerzita Palackého v Olomouci.

Peters, Pam 2015. Response to Davies and Fuchs. *English World-Wide* 36/1. 41–44.

Pettman, Charles 1913. *Africanderisms: A Glossary of South African Colloquial Words and Phrases and of Place and Other Names*. London: Longmans, Green & Co.

Pingali, Sailaja 2009. *Indian English*. Edinburgh: Edinburgh University Press.
Plag, Ingo 1999. *Morphological Productivity: Structural Constraints in English Derivation*. Berlin: Mouton de Gruyter.
Plag, Ingo 2003. *Word-Formation in English*. Cambridge: Cambridge University Press.
Plag, Ingo 2006. Productivity. In Brown, Keith (ed.) *Encyclopedia of Language and Linguistics*. Amsterdam: Elsevier. 121–128.
Pride, John B. (ed.) 1982. *New Englishes*. Rowley, MA: Newbury House.
Quirk, Randolph 1958. Linguistics. In White, Beatrice / Dorsch, T.S. (eds) *The Year's Work in English Studies, 1956*. London: Oxford University Press. 33–53.
Quirk, Randolph 2014. *Grammatical and Lexical Variance in English*. London: Routledge.
Rajagopalan, Kanavillil 1997. Linguistics and the Myth of Nativity: Comments on the Controversy over 'New/Non-native Englishes'. *Journal of Pragmatics* 27. 225–231.
Ramson, William R. 1988. *The Australian National Dictionary*. Melbourne: Oxford University Press.
Rayson, Paul 2008. From Key Words to Key Semantic Domains. *International Journal of Corpus Linguistics* 13/4. 519–549.
Reinecke, John E. 1938. Trade Jargons and Creole Dialects as Marginal Languages. *Social Forces* 17/1. 107–118.
Rey, Alain 1995. The Concept of Neologism and the Evolution of Terminologies in Individual Languages. In Sager, Juan (ed.) *Essays on Terminology*. Amsterdam: John Benjamins. Translated and edited by Sager, Juan. 9–28.
Rothman, Jason / Rell, Amy 2005. A Linguistic Analysis of Spanglish: Relating Language to Identity. *Linguistics and the Human Sciences* 1. 515–536.
Rubdy, Rani 2001. Creative Destruction: Singapore's Speak Good English Movement. *World Englishes* 20. 341–355.
Salazar, Danica 2014. Towards Improved Coverage of Southeast Asian Englishes in the *Oxford English Dictionary*. *Lexicography* 1/1. 95–108.
Salazar, Danica 2017. Release Notes: Indian English. Available at: http://public.oed.com/the-oed-today/recent-updates-to-the-oed/september-2017-update/release-notes-indian-english. (accessed 11/02/2018).
Saraceni, Mario 2014. A Response to "Researching and Critiquing World Englishes", by A. Mahboob and J. Liang. *Asian Englishes* 16/3. 259–260.
Saraceni, Mario 2015. *World Englishes: A Critical Analysis*. London: Bloomsbury.
Schmid, Hans-Jörg 2008. New Words in the Mind: Concept-Formation and Entrenchment of Neologisms. *Anglia: Zeitschrift für englische Philologie* 126/1. 1–36.
Schmid, Hans-Jörg 2014. Lexico-grammatical Patterns, Pragmatic Associations and Discourse Frequency. In Herbst, Thomas, / Schmid, Hans-Jörg / Faulhaber, Susen (eds) *Constructions. Collocations and Patterns*. Berlin: Mouton de Gruyter. 239–293.
Schmid, Hans-Jörg 2016. *English Morphology and Word-Formation: An Introduction*. 3rd ed. Berlin: Erich Schmidt.

Schmied, Josef 2004. Cultural Discourse in the Corpus of East African English and Beyond: Possibilities and Problems of Lexical and Collocational Research in a One Million-Word Corpus. *World Englishes* 23/2. 251–260.

Schmied, Josef 2006. East African Englishes. *Handbook of World Englishes*. In Kachru, Braj B. / Kachru, Yamuna / Nelson, Cecil L. (eds) London: Blackwell. 188–202.

Schneider, Edgar W. 2003. The Dynamics of New Englishes: From Identity Construction to Dialect Birth. *Language* 79/2. 233–281.

Schneider, Edgar W. 2007. *Postcolonial English*. Cambridge: Cambridge University Press.

Schneider, Edgar W. 2014. New Reflections on the Evolutionary Dynamics of World Englishes. *World Englishes* 33/1. 9–32.

Schreier, Daniel / Trudgill, Peter / Schneider, Edgar W. / Williams, Jeffrey P. (eds) 2010. *The Lesser-Known Varieties of English: An Introduction*. Cambridge: Cambridge University Press.

Schröder, Anne / Mühleisen, Susanne 2010. New Ways of Investigating Morphological Productivity. *Arbeiten aus Anglistik und Amerikanistik* 35. 43–59.

Seargeant, Philip 2010. Naming and Defining in World Englishes. *World Englishes* 29/1. 97–113.

Seargeant, Philip / Tagg, Caroline 2011. English on the Internet and a 'Post-varieties' Approach to Language. *World Englishes* 30/4. 496–514.

Seidlhofer, Barbara 2004. Research Perspectives on Teaching English as a Lingua Franca. *Annual Review of Applied Linguistics* 24. 209–239.

Seidlhofer, Barbara 2011. *Understanding English as a Lingua Franca*. Oxford: Oxford University Press.

Sharma, Devyani 2011. Style Repertoire and Social Change in British Asian English. *Journal of Sociolinguistics* 15/4. 464–492.

Silva, Penny (ed.) l998. *A Dictionary of South African English on Historical Principles*. Oxford: Oxford University Press.

Simango, Silvester R. 2006. East Africa. In Ammon, Ulrich / Dittmar, Norbert / Mattheier, Klaus / Trudgill, Peter (eds) *Sociolinguistics: An International Handbook of the Science of Language and Society. Volume 3*. Berlin: Mouton de Gruyter. 1964-1971.

Singh, Rajendra (ed.) 1998. *The Native Speaker: Multilingual Perspectives*. New Delhi: Sage.

Smead, Robert N. 1998. English Loanwords in Chicano Spanish: Characterization and Rationale. *Bilingual Review* 23/2. 113–123.

Stavans, Ilan 2000. *Dictionary of Spanglish*. New York: Basic Books.

Štekauer, Pavol 2005. Onomasiological Approach to Word-Formation. In Štekauer, Pavol / Lieber, Rochelle (eds) *Handbook of Word-Formation*. Dordrecht: Springer. 207–232.

Svartvik, Jan / Leech, Geoffrey 2016. *English: One Tongue, Many Voices*. 2nd ed. Basingstoke: Palgrave Macmillan.

Tieken-Bonn van Ostade, Ingrid 2012. The Codification of English in England. In Hickey, Raymond (ed.) *Standards of English. Codified Varieties around the World*. Cambridge: Cambridge University Press. 34–54.

References

Tweedie, Fiona / Baayen, Harald 1998. How Variable May a Constant Be? Measure of Lexical Richness in Perspective. *Journal of Quantitative Linguistics* 32/5. 323–352.

van Rooy, Bertus 2006. The Extension of Progressive Aspect in Black South African English. *World Englishes* 25. 37–64.

van Rooy, Bertus 2010. Social and Linguistic Perspectives on Variability in World Englishes. *World Englishes* 29. 3–20.

van Rooy, Bertus / Terblanche, Lize 2010. Complexity in Word-Formation Processes in New Varieties of South African English, *Southern African Linguistics and Applied Language Studies* 28/4. 357–374.

Veale, Tony / Butnariu, Cristina 2010. Harvesting and Understanding On-line Neologisms. In Onysko, Alexander / Michel, Sascha (eds) *Cognitive Perspectives on Word Formation*. New York: de Gruyter. 393–416.

Webster, Noah 1828. *An American Dictionary of the English Language*. New York: S. Converse.

Wee, Lionel 2004. Reduplication and Discourse Particles. In Lim, Lisa (ed.) *Singapore English*. Amsterdam/Philadelphia: John Benjamins. 105–126.

Wei, Li 1998. The 'Why' and 'How' Questions in the Analysis of Conversational Code Switching. In Auer, Peter (ed.) *Code Switching in Conversation: Language, Interaction and Identity*. London, UK: Routledge. 156–176.

Whitworth, George Clifford 1885. *Anglo-Indian Dictionary: A Glossary of Such Indian Terms Used in English, and Such English or Other Non-Indian Terms as have Obtained Special Meanings in India*. London: Kegan Paul, Trench & Co.

Wilkins, David P. 1996. Natural Tendencies of Semantic Change and the Search for Cognates. In Durie, Mark / Ross, Malcolm (eds) *The Comparative Method Reviewed*. Oxford: Oxford University Press. 264–306.

Winford, Donald 2010. Contact and Borrowing. In Hickey, Raymond (ed.) *The Handbook of Language Contact*. Oxford: Blackwell. 170–187.

Young, Simon N. 2006. A Rant against Jargon and Neologisms. *Journal of Psychiatry & Neuroscience* 31/3. 155–156.

Zentella, Ana Celia 2008. Preface. In Niño-Murcia, Mercedes / Rothman, Jason (eds) *Bilingualism and Identity: Spanish at the Crossroads with Other Languages*. Amsterdam, Philadelphia, PA: John Benjamins. 3–9.

Index

Figures given in *italics*, Tables in **bold** and Notes by page number, 'n', note number(s).

abbreviations 48–49
acquisition of language 24
acrolectal languages 115, 117
acronyms 49; Indian English 113; Nigerian English 75; Philippine English 108; Singaporean English 92, 95
ad hoc word formations 130
Adedimeji, Mahfouz A. 73
Adegbija, Efurosibina 72, 78
adjective compounds 106
affixation 47–48; Indian English 113; macrovarieties 120; Nigerian English 73; South African English 87
Africa, English in 69–88
African language research 62
Afrikaans words 86
agentive suffixes 47–48
Ajani, Timothy T. 74
Alabi, Victoria A. 78
Algeo, John 46, 48–49
alphabetisms *see* initialisms
alternation 100
ameliorations 51
American Dictionary of the English Language 61
American English: borrowings 50; *bungalow* term 124; indigenous languages 50, 52n7; sub-varieties of 103; use of term 52n6
anti-standard ethos 27
appropriation processes 128
archaic meanings, preserving 71

'archaism' 41
ASEAN countries 121
Asian varieties 62, 88–115, 121, 124
Association of Southeast Asian Nations *see* ASEAN countries
'aterritorial' concept 120, 131
AUE *see* Australian English
Australian dictionaries 61
Australian English (AUE) 49
automatic processes, neologisms 53

backclipping 49
back-formation 92
backronyms 49
Bajan language 115
Bamgbose, Ayo 71–72
Bamiro, Edmund 72
Barnhart, David K. 40
bases 47
basilectal languages 116, 117
Bauer, Laurie 37, 42, 47, 50
Belize 119–120
Biermeier, Thomas 106–108
big-data-based corpora 56
Black South African English (BSAE) 85
blending 49–50; Nigerian English 73, 79; Singaporean English 92
blogs, corpora 58
Bokamba, Eyamba 70, 71
Booij, Geert 37–38, 129
borrowings 45, 50–51; code-mixing link 100; Hong Kong English

101, 103; Indian English 114;
  Singaporean English 91–94, 99–100
braai word frequency 87, **88**
brinjal term 110, **110**
Brown, Adam 91–92
BSAE *see* Black South African English
Buang, Sri Norazrin 93–94
Budohoska, Natalia 81
bungalow term 124
Buregeya, Alfred 80
bwana loanword 80, **81**

calques 50
Caribbean dictionaries 61
Caribbean English 62, 115–120
categorizations and models 14–23
CCJ *see* Corpus of Cyber-Jamaican
Chinese language, borrowings from 93, 101, **101**, 103
chronological criterion, definitions 11
Circles of English model 19
clipping 49; Indian English 113; Jamaican English 118; Singaporean English 92, 98
clothes, words for 74
code-mixing 99–100
code-switching 99
codification: concept of 6–7; dictionaries 85; legitimization and 132; neologisms 85; standard varieties 28
cognitive consolidation, neologisms 42
cognitive recognition 39, 44
coinages: African English 70, 71–72; Philippine English 108–109; Singaporean English 92–93
Colloquial Singapore English (CSGE) 90, **94**
colonial era, effects of 104
comfort room term 106, **107**
community acceptance: neologisms 42; word formations 37
comparative data 55, 62–63
complex system, English as 27
complexity, South African English 85
composites 47–48
compounding 48; Indian variety 111–114; Jamaican English 118; Philippine English 106; Singaporean English 92, 93, 96

congruent lexicalization 100
contact languages 28–30; Caribbean 115–116; Singaporean English 90
contamination, World Englishes 128–129
contextual identification, neologisms 44
contextual importance, Singaporean varieties 91
continuum concept 90, 116–117
contrastive analyses 25
conventionalization process 43–44
conversion 51, 92
coordinative compounds 106, 118
copulative compounds 48
corpora: methodologies 54–60; research approach 64; use of 4, 38, 131–132
Corpus of Cyber-Jamaican (CCJ) 117
Corpus of Global Web-based English *see* GLoWbE
creativity 36–38; blending and 79; definition 36; word formation 129–131
creoles 28–30, *29*, 115–117
cross-contamination processes 124
cross-fertilization processes 127, 129, 132–133
CSGE *see* Colloquial Singapore English
cultural aspects: nativeness 24–25; Singaporean words 91
cultural restrictions 120–121
cum preposition 96–98, **97**, 107, 111

daily life, words for 92
data sources, corpora as 58
'de-territorial' concept 120
definitional issues 11–13
deliberate coinage 70
"deliberate satirical neologisms" 79
derivation: affixes 47; East African English 83–84; Singaporean English 92; South African English 86
descriptive patterns, codification 7
diachronic criteria, neologisms 39
diachronic languages 100–101
dialect concept 27–28, 51
diaspora of languages 27
dictionaries: entering words 130–131; Jamaican English 126n33; labeling

Index 155

items **123**, 132; lexicographic aspect 39; methodological approach 60–62; neologisms in 40; research approach 63–64; South Africa 85–86
dictionary codification 85
differentiation, dynamic models 16
diglossia concept 116
discourse perspectives 100
diversification, level of 7
domestication of language 79–80
Dumay, Nicolas 44
Dutch language 115
Dynamic Model of PCE 14–16
dynamism of languages 6, 17, 39, 128

EAE *see* East African English
East Africa 80–84
East African English (EAE) 69, 80, 83–84, 86, 125n8
education, effects of 26
-ee suffix 107–108
EFL *see* English as a Foreign Language
EIF framework *see* Extra- and Intra-territorial Forces framework
ELF *see* English as a Lingua Franca
emic perspective, research 65
endocentric compounds 48
endonormative processes, modeling 18
endonormative stabilization 16
endoproductive importance, neologisms 63
'English', notion of 127
'English compound' 10
English as a Foreign Language (EFL) 12, 16–17
'English language complex' 10
English lexicon, definition 36
English as a Lingua Franca (ELF) 11, 13, 18
English as a Native Language (ENL) 17
English as a Second Language (ESL) 12, 16–17
ENL *see* English as a Native Language
entrenchment-and-conventionalization framework 44
eponyms 52
ESL *see* English as a Second Language
establishment process, neologisms 42
Evans, Stephen 100–101
exocentric compounds 48

exonormative stabilization 15
exoproductive importance, neologism 63
expressions, creation of 38
extension, semantic: African English 70; East African English 83; Jamaican English 118; Nigerian English 76–77
Extra- and Intra-territorial Forces (EIF) framework 16

family words 77, 118
Filipino language 104–105, 136–138, *see also* Philippine English
flora, words for 75
food: Indian words for 110; Nigerian words for 74–75; Singaporean words for 91
foreclipping 49
formal neology 51
foundation stage, dynamic models 15
French language 115
frequency studies: lexemes 66n10; loanwords 80, **81**, **82**; regional varieties 58–59; use of 64–65

Gaskell, Gareth 44
generalization 78
'generification' process 52
geographical criterion, modeling 17
geographical heterogeneity 62
gestalt concept 44
global language, English as 12–13, 19–20
Glocal English 12
GLoWbE (Corpus of Global Web-based English) 54–56, **57**, 58–59; loanwords 80, **81**, **82**; macrovarieties 121; research approach 62; structural descriptions 131
Görlach, Manfred 36
Graddol, David 20
grammatical structures 100
guanxi term **102**, 103

handphone term 124
hapax legomenon 64
Hickey, Raymond 26
hierarchical power, standards 14
Hindi words 114
historical processes, definitions 11

156 *Index*

HKE *see* Hong Kong English
Honey, John 26
Hong Kong English (HKE) 100–103; frequency in corpora 59; *kiasu* term 93; log-likelihood of items **60**; OED updates 2016 134–135
hybrid compounds 112
hypernyms 48
hypostatization 42

ICE (International Corpus of English) 54–55, **56**, 58–59; research approach 62; structural descriptions 131
identity traits, local languages 12
ideological constructs 26
idioms 72, 78–79
Igbo words 73, 124n4
independent parallel development hypothesis 29
India, English in 109–115
Indian communities, South Africa 87
Indian English (INE) 109–110, 113–114, 124; corpora studies 59; dictionaries 61; log-likelihood of items **59**
indigenous languages, America 50, 52n7
INE *see* Indian English
infixes 47
inflection 47
initialisms 49, 75, 95
innovation processes 129–131
insertion 100
institutionalization, neologisms 42–43
integrative approaches 31
intelligibility in models 21–22
interethnic lingua francas 71
interim word formations 130
International Corpus of English *see* ICE
Internet use 54, 58, 60, 64, *see also* web-derived corpora
intervarietal borrowings 45
intervarietal word formation 43

Jamaican Creole (JC) 115–117, 119, 126n35
Jamaican English (JE) 116–120, 126n33
JC *see* Jamaican Creole
JE *see* Jamaican English
jeepney term 106, **108**

Kaan, Aondover Theophilus 76, 78
Kachru, Braj B. 15
Kachruvian model 17–19
Kenyan English (KEE) 69, 80–82
Kenyanisms 81
kiasu term 93
Kishwahili 80, 82
kuya term 105, **105**

labeling: in dictionaries 132; macrovarieties 122–124, **123**; word formations 4
language, conceptualization 30
language boundaries/borders 3, 128
language corpora 4, *see also* corpora
language systems/networks 129
language usage, lexicographic authority 61
Leech, Geoffrey 84
Leimgruber, Jakob R. E. 94
lemmas: dictionary resources 60, 63; macrovarietal 122
lesser-known varieties 11–12, 127
Levchenko, Yaroslav 53
lexemes: acceptance of 43–44; definition 44n1; frequencies 66n10; Indian English 110, 112
lexical/idiomatic processes distinction 78–79
lexicalization, neologisms 42–43, 44
lexico-semantic reinvestment 76
lexicographic criteria, neologisms 39
lexicographic labels 122–124
'lexicon' concept 35–36
lingua franca phenomenon 13, 70–71
linguo-cultural borrowing 73
literature, Nigerian English 71, 72
loanwords 45, 50, 52n4-5, 52n8; East African English 80–81; Hong Kong English 101
local languages: as identity trait 12; investigation of 19–20; Nigeria 73
log-likelihood values **59**, **60**
Loureiro-Porto, Lucia 58, 60
Low, Ee Ling 91–92

McArthur, Tom 15, 19, 28
macrovarietal approach 120–126, 132
makan term **94**

Malaysian English (MYE): borrowings from 93–94; lexical items **122**, 124; reduplication 99; Singaporean English similarities 125n14
media effects 25, *see also* Internet; press use
mesolectal languages 116, 117
Metcalf, Allan 40
Milroy, Jim 26
models 14–23, 129, *see also* categorizations and models
modifications: dictionary terms 39; idioms 72
monocentric models 128
monogentic hypothesis 29
monolingualism 24
monolithic constructs 23
morphological issues, word formations 35
morphological productivity 37–38
mother tongue, construct of 23
multilingual contexts 23–24
music, words for 74
MYE *see* Malaysian English

narrowing, semantic 77–78
native/non-native varieties distinction 127
native speakers categorization 21, 23–25
nativeness 8, 23–25, 37
nativization, definitions 15
nautical jargon hypothesis 29
NE *see* Nigerian English
'necrologisms' 41
negative connotations, Singlish 90–91
negative prefixation 87
Nelson, Gerald 131
neoclassical compounds 48
"neological continuum" 41
neologisms 3, 38–40; analysis of 130; approaches to 53–54; codification 85; corpora relationship 64; definition 45–46; evolution of 8, 60; formation of 45, 50; Nigerian English 73, 79; nonce-formations and 40–44; research questions 63; semantic drift 51; South African English **86**; use of 4
New Englishes 11, 29–30
Newmark, Peter 45–46
newness in language 39

Nigerian English (NE) 69, 70–80
Nigerian Pidgin English (NPE) 70–71
non-morphematic word formations 45
non-native language users 21, 25, 37
non-native/native varieties distinction 127
non-standard English 27, 71
nonce-formations 40–44, 64
normation process, neologisms 43
nouns, *kiasu* term 93
NPE *see* Nigerian Pidgin English

O'Donovan, Ruth 53
OED *see* Oxford English Dictionary
O'Neil, Mary 53
Oxford English Dictionary (OED) 60–61; Filipino language updates 136–138; Hong Kong English updates 134–135; Tagalog language updates 136–138
Ozón, Gabriel 131

Papiamento 115
paradigm evolution 128–129
parallel development hypothesis 29
particle compounds 48
patoi/patwa *see* Jamaican Creole
PCE *see* Postcolonial Englishes
pejorations 51
performance levels, native/non-native speakers 24
Philippine English (PHE) 89, **89**, 103–109, **122**, *see also* Filipino language
pickney term 118
pidgins 28–30; Caribbean 115, 116; Nigerian 70–71
Pingali, Sailaja 113
Plag, Ingo 47–51
pluricentric models 20–21, 128–129
polycentric models *21*, 22
polysemous words 118
Postcolonial Englishes (PCE) 11, 14–16
post-geopolitical varieties 120
'postlogisms' 41
'post-WE integrative approach' 31
potentiality 37
prefixation 47, 83, 87
prelogisms 41

158 Index

prescriptive approach, standards 25–27
prescriptive patterns, codification 7
press use, neologisms 53–54
productivity 36–38, 53
proficiency: levels of 109; polycentric model 21–23
protologisms 41
prototypical compounds 48
psychological criteria, neologisms 39

quadrangulation *65*

reciprocal contamination 128–129
reduplication 78, 98–99
regional varieties 19–20; East African English 84; frequency studies 58–59; potential of 132
religion, words for 75, 91
research approaches 30–31, 62–65
roots 47
rule-governed creativity/productivity 36, 129

sabir language 29
SAE *see* South African English
Salazar, Danica 121–122, 131
salwar term 112
"satirical neologisms" 79
Schmid, Hans-Jörg 42, 44, 48
Schneider, Edgar W. 16
semantic autonomy 42
semantic criteria, neologisms 39
semantic drift 51
semantic extension: African English 70; East African English 83; Jamaican English 118; Nigerian English 76–77
semantic narrowing 77–78
semantic neology 51
semantic reduplication 78
semantic shifts: African English 70, 71; Indian words 110–111; Nigerian English 78
semantic transfer 70
semantic variation: Nigerian English 76, 79; Philippine English 108; Singaporean English 94–95
Singapore, languages 90–100
Singaporean English (SGE) 59, **59**, 89; approaches to 94–95; definition 90; lexical items **122**; Malaysian English similarities 125n14; word formations 89, 91–96
Singlish 90–91
situational context, Singaporean varieties 91
slang words 119–120
social plane, neologisms 44
social practice, language as 127
sociocultural aspects: nativeness 24–25; neologisms 130
sociological perspectives 5
South African Concise Oxford Dictionary 85–86
South African English (SAE) 61, 69, 84–88, 124
South Asia 114–115
South-East Asian English 121, 124
Southern African English 69, *see also* South African English
Spanglish 50, 52n3
Spanish language 115
SPICE Ireland 55, 65n5
spoken English: ICE project 55, 58; Jamaica 116, 117; written English distinction 26
SSGE *see* Standard Singapore English
Standard English 26, 128
'Standard Indian English' 109
Standard Jamaican English 117
Standard Singapore English (SSGE) 90
standardization/standard varieties: criteria 25–30; definition 27–28; descriptive meaning 7; dictionaries 61; hierarchical power 14; level of 6; Nigerian English 71; World Englishes 5
statistics 10
status, standard notion 25, 26
stems 47
stokvel term 86, 125n11
structural descriptions, corpora 131
suffixation 47–48; East African English 83–84; Jamaican English 119; Philippine English 107–108
supranational form, written English 26
Svartvik, Jan 84
synthetic compounds 106, 112–113

Tagalog language 104–105, 136–138
Tanzanian English (TZE) 69, 80

tautological formations 78
technological changes, effects of 4
Terblanche, Lize 85, 87
territorial analysis 131
topicality, lexemes 43
transfer, semantic 70
transnational polycentrism *21*, 22
Trinbagonian language 115
tsotsi term 86, 125n12
TZE *see* Tanzanian English

Ugandan English 80, 84
uhuru loanword 80, **82**
universalist hypotheses 29
unpredictability, creative process 37
Urdu language 114

van Rooy, Bertus 85, 87
variations: Nigerian English 76, 79; Philippine English 108; Singaporean English 94–95; word formation 35
varietal labels 122–124, 132
variety concept 27–28, 127
vernacular languages, Nigeria 71
vocabulary: borrowing and 114; slang words 120; varieties of English 36

WE *see* World Englishes
'WE-ness' concept 18–19
web-derived corpora 55, 132, *see also* Internet use
Wee, Lionel 98
West African English 69, 71, *see also* Nigerian English

wet market term 103, **103**
White South African English (WSEA) 85
WIE *see* 'World International English'
'word': clarification of term 35; life cycle stages *41*
word formations: African English 70; Asian varieties **89**, 90–96; creativity/innovation 129–131; cross-fertilization 127; East African English 83; intervarietal issues 43; labeling 4; neologisms 8, 38; Nigerian English 71; processes 45–52; productivity of 37, 38; sociological perspective 5; technological changes 4; variations 35; varietal identification 63
World Englishes movement 128
World Englishes (WE): approaches to 13, 29–30; assumptions about 127; concept of 129; corpus materials 54; creativity in 130; ethos 30–31; growth/influence 4
'World International English' (WIE) 13
'World Standard English' (WSE) 13
'World System of Englishes' model 14
World System of Standard and Non-standard Englishes 14, **15**
written English: ICE project 55; spoken English distinction 26
WSE *see* 'World Standard English'
WSEA *see* White South African English

yaardie term 118–119

For Product Safety Concerns and Information please contact our EU representative GPSR@taylorandfrancis.com
Taylor & Francis Verlag GmbH, Kaufingerstraße 24, 80331 München, Germany

www.ingramcontent.com/pod-product-compliance
Lightning Source LLC
Chambersburg PA
CBHW051646230426
43669CB00013B/2465